ET 13812   6

COMMUNITY EDUCATION:
FROM PROGRAM TO PROCESS

COMMUNITY EDUCATION:
FROM PROGRAM TO PROCESS

**Jack D. Minzey
and
Clyde LeTarte**

PENDELL
PUBLISHING
COMPANY

Internation Standard Book Number: 0-87812-040-8
Library of Congress Catalog Card Number: 76-189279

©1972 by
Pendell Publishing Company
Midland, Michigan

All Rights Reserved
Published 1972
Second Printing 1973
Printing in the United States of America

To our wives, Esther and Kathy

CONTENTS

SECTION I   THE COMMUNITY EDUCATION CONCEPT

Chapter I   Community Education:
What It Is and Is Not 3

Chapter II   Moving From Program to Process 31

SECTION II   INITIATING AND DEVELOPING COMMUNITY EDUCATION

Chapter III   Implementing the Concept 45

Chapter IV   Organizing a Community for Process 63

SECTION III   PROGRAM DEVELOPMENT

Chapter V   Adult Education 81

Chapter VI   Recreation 117

Chapter VII   Student Enrichment 127

Chapter VIII   Public Relations and Community Education . 135

SECTION IV   STAFFING FOR COMMUNITY EDUCATION

Chapter IX   Determining and Meeting Staffing Needs ... 161

Chapter X   Establishing an In-Service Program to
Meet Staff Needs..................... 179

CONTENTS (Cont'd)

SECTION V   ECONOMIC CONSIDERATIONS IN COMMUNITY EDUCATION

Chapter XI   Including the Economic Sector of the Community 195

Chapter XII   Financing Community Education 203

Chapter XIII   Establishing a Budget 215

SECTION VI   PLANNING FOR FACILITY IMPROVEMENT, EVALUATION AND THE FUTURE

Chapter XIV   School Plant Planning 229

Chapter XV   Evaluation 241

Chapter XVI   The Future of Community Education 263

SECTION I

The Community Education Concept

CHAPTER I

Community Education: What It Is and Is Not

The primary step in the examination of any subject is the definition of terms to clarify the guidelines of the inquiry and to assure that those involved are proceeding from a common base. Consequently, any discussion of Community Education should include an examination of the meaning of the term "Community Education."

Unfortunately, the strengths and weaknesses of Community Education have often been examined without this basic step. As a result, Community Education has suffered more from misconceptions and misunderstandings than for any other reason. Many activities have been falsely labeled as Community Education, and many Community Education persons have promoted as Community Education things which fall short of the complete definition. Consequently, Community Educators have frequently had to defend their existence in the light of false conceptions and misunderstandings about the true meaning of Community Education and its potential.

Before attempting the task of defining Community Education, it might first be more appropriate to discuss some of the more popular misconceptions of Community Education and identify what Community Education "is not." In trying to point out the differences between Community Education and its misnomers, one thread of consistency is notable, namely, that, in general those things which are often called Community Education are usually only portions of Community Education. Thus, proponents of Community Education are often settling for less than the total gestalt of Community Education without acknowledging this fact.

Programs

The most frequent misconception is between the concept of Community Education and its programs. Community Education is the over-arching conceptual base, while programs are the activities related to the solution of specific community needs. Thus, enrichment opportunities, recreation programs, cultural activities, avocational offerings, and political and civic programs are partial ways of resolving certain community problems. "Too frequently, a well-intentioned program based on the concept of Community Education has culminated in evening activities for adults. This occurs because the personnel involved in such situations possess a vague understanding of the depth and ramifications of the Community Education concept. The most important aspect of Community Education is not *program* but *process*. It is the relationship between these two terms which is fundamental to the concept of Community Education. The ultimate goal of Community Education is to develop a process by which members of a community learn to work together to identify problems and to seek out solutions to these problems. It is through this process that an on-going procedure is established for working together on all community issues . . . . .

Programs are those overt activities which are designed to resolve the issues identified by the process . . . . . Failure of Community Education efforts are often the result of excessive emphasis on programs with little or no attention to the process of Community Development."[1]

In fairness to those who do strive for total Community Education but end up primarily with programs, it should be noted that

---

[1]Howard Hickey, Curt Van Voorhees, and Associated, *The Role of the School in Community Education,* Pendell Publishing Co., Midland, Michigan, 1969, p. 36.

Community Education: What It Is and Is Not

Community Education is generally achieved in two stages. The first stage is often highly program-oriented and comes about as a result of meeting the immediate more obvious needs as perceived by the community. Local citizens and agencies will often demand to see programs in operation soon after Community Education is implemented. An abundance of programs will often meet some community needs through greater use of facilities by providing activities, and by emulating what community members have seen in other communities. It will also assist those responsible for Community Education in getting people more actively and overtly into programs and provide additional access for getting them further involved. True Community Education is endangered when the community or the directors of Community Education become so obsessed and encumbered with programs that they are either unable or unwilling to proceed to the second stage which is community process and community self-actualization.

Neighborhood School

Many people perceive Community Education and the neighborhood school concept as the same thing. The biggest problem with this misconception is the connotation that the term *"neighborhood schools"* has carried in the past. Schools do play an important part in the Community Education concept as advocated by most experts in Community Education; and the school building, as a neighborhood center, plays a key role in providing facilities and serving as a unifying force in identifying *community*. The term *neighborhood school*, however, has been used frequently in the past in connection with racial segregation. It has been used to support segregation on the basis that students, due to convenience and other advantages, should attend the schools in their immediate neighborhood. As a result, *de jure* integration was circumvented by *de facto* segregation on the basis of housing patterns. This usage of the term has negated its positive use with the black community and as a result, conjurs up many ominous perceptions which doom Community Education before it begins.

It is true that Community Education seeks to develop a sense of community in the neighborhood and to use the local schools for programs. Its success, however, is not dependent upon the attendance of the school age students at specific schools. Thus, Community Education might function very effectively even in a district which had endorsed bussing of students for integration purposes.

Community Education: From Program to Process

Many critics of Community Education have referred to it as a relic of the past; the neighborhood school concept with a new title. These same critics go on to state that as such it is not meeting the modern day societal problems that the educational system must face and is, instead, an attempt to maintain the status quo.

The neighborhood school, in this traditional sense, is simply a school within a local community or neighborhood that is readily accessible to its constituents because of its proximity. It is normally perceived as an elementary school within easy walking distance of most children; its purpose being the education of these same children. This approach to education has become controversial because some people believe that it is a means of maintaining segregation and a segregated educational system. Because the school serves the surrounding community under this plan, and because segregation is usually most evident in housing patterns, the schools often mirror the ethnic distribution of the neighborhood and thus provide the basis for this criticism. As a result of present housing patterns, black communities tend to have black schools and white neighborhoods tend to have white schools. Critics believe that this condition compounds the problem of segregation and tends to thwart attempts toward integration.

It is the contention of the authors that the concept of Community Education and the neighborhood school are not the same, and the two are only similar in that both use the local elementary school as the basic unit of the total educational system. Further, it is our belief that because of the basic tenets of Community Education — citizen involvement, sharing of decision-making, and total community involvement in the education enterprize — that the possibilities of true integration for the total society are greatly enhanced through acceptance of this philosophy.

The very essence of Community Education is a belief that the school is most effective when it involves the people it is attempting to serve in designing the program and opportunities that the educational system is going to provide. Because large scale involvement is believed essential, the neighborhood school becomes the one unit that can be utilized as a basis of operations. It is the one facility that all neighborhoods have in common. No other agency or governmental system has a structural framework that approaches that available through the local elementary school, and it is the only governmental

Community Education: What It Is and Is Not

agency that exists in neighborhoods all over the country. This accessibility alone provides the very best opportunities possible for true grass roots involvement. Further, the educational system as a system, is the one remaining unit that is common to all groups in our society that can bind and pull the very diverse elements within our society together and begin working toward some positive goals — goals perceived as worthwhile by a large number of people who are willing to work together to achieve them.

Community Control

Community control has become one of the controversial educational terms that engenders great animosity or support from various groups and individuals. The term is often used synonymously with decentralization and community involvement as well as Community Education.

Community control, as the word *control* implies, delegates the responsibility and the decision-making authority concerning the educational system to the constituent citizenry — the grass roots local residents. Lay citizens totally control the operation of the school and the education of their children, and are responsible for all decisions from trivia to major policy determinations.

The move toward an educational system based upon community control is based upon several motivational factors:

1. There is a feeling, especially in districts with large educational systems, that local needs and local concerns are not only not being met by educators, they are being virtually ignored. Community control is perceived as a method of reversing this situation and providing individuals access to decision-makers within the educational institution.

2. Many of the more militant factions of the black community believe that the polarization of races and their regrouping as an ethnic body must take place before meaningful integration can ever occur. One of the ways that this can be accomplished is through educational systems controlled by the community and reflecting the educational programs that they believe are neces-

sary. Incorporated into this thinking is a total rejection of the involvement of the present structure, resulting from mistrust and past negative experiences.

3. There is a general belief that many of our social problems result from a highly bureaucratic, systematized, formalized operational pattern that stifles creative thinking and squelches disagreement and healthy dissent. This group generally believes that the answer to this problem has to be the elimination of the "system," replacing it with meaningful individual and group participation; the involvement of the lay citizen being the single most crucial need for the growth and development of a new responsive system. The concept of community control was brought to light in very practical terms with the problems and conflict created in the Ocean-Hill Brownsville system.

The Ocean-Hill Brownsville Experiment

Because community control is now identified with Ocean-Hill Brownsville, a brief review of this case is beneficial to a basic understanding of the issue involved.

In an article in the April, 1969, issue of *Phi Delta Kappan,* Mario Fantini and Marilyn Gittell describe the situation surrounding the Ocean-Hill Brownsville situation.[2] Several major factors caused the immense conflict that gained national attention. First, the creation of the district in the summer of 1967 was accomplished in the midst of controversy, misunderstandings, and intense emotionalism. It was the result of a school board attempting to meet demands for increased community participation and a desire to improve the educational opportunities of the children in the area.

Nat Henthoff explained that much of the conflict was caused by a total lack of trust between the school board and the local residents. In 1958, the school board had promised that the proposed new intermediate school, 201, would be an integrated quality school. In the

---

[2] Mario Fantini and Marilyn Gittell, "The Ocean-Hill Brownsville Experiment," *Phi Delta Kappan,* Vol. L, No. 8, April, 1969, pp. 442-445.

spring of 1966, the local superintendent told parents that this promised integration would be accomplished through a 50-50 mix — 50 percent Negro and 50 percent Puerto Rican.[3] The community felt that they had been deceived and reacted by opposing any further efforts to work with the administration.

It seems evident that the goal of community involvement was transformed by mistrust and alienation into a goal of administrator exclusion. What started as a positive step toward meaningful community involvement ended with a desire to virtually exclude the professional educators within the system. Community involvement had become community control, with a major emphasis upon hiring and firing rights and separation from the larger administrative structure.

It is suggested here that Ocean-Hill Brownsville should not be considered a prototype of community control and certainly not an example of positive and meaningful community involvement. At best, it exemplifies the results of not having a program of meaningful community involvement and a plan to incorporate community needs and concerns into the decision-making process.

Educators must share the decision-making process in educational programming and involve lay citizens in the process of formulating policies and procedures. This not only will avoid the problems described in the Ocean-Hill Brownsville case, it will also assure a more meaningful and relevant educational program. If Ocean-Hill Brownsville has a lesson to give, it is this: educators cannot afford to force people into extreme positions to gain a voice in the educational system. When this happens there is a tendency to eliminate the professional educator and the very valuable contribution that he must make if quality education is to be assured. Continued rejection of the community in educational matters will result in rejection of educators by the community in educational matters. Community involvement must be a joint undertaking and approached on the assumption that both lay citizens and professional educators have a unique and valuable contribution to make and each, because of their uniqueness, cannot develop an adequate educational program without the other.

---

[3] Nat Henthoff, "Making Public Schools Accountable: A Case Study of P.S. 201," *Phi Delta Kappan,* March, 1967, pp. 332-335, Vol. XLIII, No. 7.

Community Education: From Program to Process

In general terms, the phrase *community control* implies a truism which should exist in every school district. Legally, control of education is vested in the states, but most people subscribe to the idea that control of education should reside in locally elected boards of education who are responsive to the needs of the community. As a result of recent developments, community control has tended to be associated with decentralization and more specifically the Ocean-Hill Brownsville incident has come to mean control over the educational operation of such things as curriculum, policy-making, and employment of staff, rather than involvement of community in the decision-making process of schools. As a result, it does not seem to be a more viable method of involving community as much as one of substituting one special interest group for another to the exclusion of other groups who need to be involved. As such, community control does not deal with community involvement, community process, or problems diverse enough to be classified as Community Education.

Poverty and Disadvantaged Programs

Many well-meaning social engineers attempt to relate Community Education only to the needs of the poor. Since Community Education has as a goal the solution of community problems, the assumption would seem to be that affluent communities have no problems. Few, if any, would acknowledge this, and in fact, one could make quite a case to show that many problems of the poor (i.e., single parent families, drugs, juvenile delinquency, etc.) are equally prevalent in the affluent segment of our society, even if not for the same reasons. In a like manner, much of our youthful activism is generating from all economic levels in our society. If these are not reasons enough to prove the point we might listen to the advice of Dr. Ernest O. Melby who states that in our prosperous communities we cannot give our people a sense of social responsibility and compassion "unless we get out of the schoolhouse, unless we bring people together around great ideas, unless we give children and their parents a chance to meet and work with people of other races and economic positions, unless the people and their children have a chance to act and give of themselves in the improvement of life of others."[4]

---

[4] Hickey, *op. cit.*

Community Education: What It Is and Is Not

Thus, there are needs in every community for Community Education. And whether it be for overt programs for children and adults, for a better understanding of the cultural differences between segments of our society, or for the solution of community problems within the community, Community Education has proved to be of value to all types of communities, regardless of the socio-economic factors of the community itself.

Social Work

In an effort to compensate for the overemphasis on programs, some community educators have promoted a technique which seeks to give more attention to community social needs, and subsequently results in an exaggerated sociological orientation to local problems. While this may be a necessary device for solving some of the community's problems, it is not an adequate substitute for Community Education. The case study approach is not the same as community development brought about through the Community Education process.

Community School

The difference between Community Education and community school is that Community Education is the concept and community school is the delivery system for that concept. Philosophically, Community Education is concerned with the many problems of a community and ways of solving those problems through community action. The community school, because of its unique location and facility, becomes a base for that action. Community Education, then, is the over-arcing concept and the community school is the device, the system which provides for the carrying out of this concept.

The question has often been raised as to why the school should serve this role. The implication is that some other agency might more effectively serve as the catalyst to promote Community Education. The fact is that some communities have tried using other agencies for this purpose. Unfortunately, this approach has not met with great success. Failure has usually resulted from a combination of certain problems which have developed. For one thing, other agencies, and particularly

Community Education: From Program to Process

those of a governmental nature, have an involvement in the political realm to a degree that is not found within the school system. This involvement results in political pressures which are given a higher priority by the governing board than are community needs. Thus, Community Education becomes secondary to political issues and is consequently less objective and effective than it is capable of being.

A second problem has been the relation of such an agency to other agencies. To attempt to institute a community agency which will have authority, even if only in a coordinating capacity, over other agencies and governmental units, is a problem of the greatest magnitude. At best, it will take a considerable amount of time and salesmanship to earn acceptablility and legitimacy for any community agency to play the coordinating role in Community Education among its peers. More specifically, as this role is identified, it becomes more apparent that many of the responsibilities taken on by the new agency are a duplication of some of the roles which the school is or should be carrying out.

A third problem is related to financing. Community Education does require a sizable budget. Some of these funds will come from other agencies and some from public monies. There is a great reluctance on the part of existing agencies to provide funds to a peer agency or some political unit of government. In addition, existing tax laws make it unwise for other funding sources, such as business, industry and, particularly, foundations, to give money to any group without a special government tax exemption. Under current regulations, public schools are usually one of the few community institutions which automatically have such an exemption.

The public school, then, has proved to be the best organization for serving as the coordinating, facilitating device for the development and implementation of Community Education. It provides an appropriate facility for many of the programs of Community Education. In addition, as a public tax-supported agency which has a common denominator through the children of the community, it is the most acceptable, nonthreatening institution to the citizens and other agencies within the community. Its strategic location also puts it in a position to most adequately serve workable portions of the population. The main point to be emphasized, however, is that Community Education is the concept and the community school is the vehicle by which the potential of the concept is most effectively realized.

In summary, we have been looking at things which have been misconceived as Community Education. In some cases, the problem has been that portions of Community Education, such as programs, social work or the community school, have been viewed as being synonymous with the total concept. In other cases, the label Community Education has been used to identify activities which are alien to the concept of Community Education such as segregated neighborhood schools. The unfortunate result has been that many things which are not Community Education in its entirety have been promoted as Community Education and this has culminated in misunderstandings and unjust criticisms about the concept of Community Education.

Defining Community Education

In order to define Community Education, one should first look at the meaning of the words which make up the term. The word *community* must be viewed as a feeling rather than a geographical characteristic in order to effectively realize its potency. It is through the interrelationships in a community that Community Education realizes its power.

"The point to be emphasized is that a community is not merely a political unit or a geographic unit or a commercial unit; it is pre-eminently a social unit. Thus, ... we may say that a community consists of people who live in a more or less contiguous area and are engaged in such social processes and relationships as may normally arise in the pursuit of the chief concerns of life."[5]

The term *community* is here being used to refer to a local situation. It implies closeness which might be characterized by a neighborhood. It also implies people who have common problems and common goals. And looking at the word *common* one should note the relationship to this total discussion.

---

[5] Edward G. Olsen, *The School and Community Reader,* The Macmillan Co., New York, 1963, p. 362.

Community Education: From Program to Process

"There is more than a verbal tie between the words *common, community,* and *communication.* Men live in a *community* in virtue of the things which they have in common; and *communication* is the way in which they come to possess things in *common.* What they must have in common in order to form a community or society are aims, beliefs, aspirations, knowledge – a common understanding – like-mindedness as the sociologists say. Such things cannot be passed physically from one to another like bricks. They cannot be shared as persons would share a pie by dividing it into physical pieces. The communication which insures participation in a common understanding is one which secures similar emotional and intellectual dispositions – like ways of responding to expectations and requirements.

Persons do not become a society by living in physical proximity, any more than *a man ceases to be socially influenced* by being so many feet or miles removed from others. A book or letter may institute a more intimate association between human beings separated thousands of miles from each other than exists between dwellers under the same roof. Individuals do not even compose a social group because they all work for a common end. The parts of a machine work with a maximum of cooperativeness for a common result, but they do not form a community. If, however, they were all cognizant of the common end and all interested in it so that they regulated their specific activity in view of it, then they would form a community. But this would involve communication. Each would have to know what the other was about and would have to have some way of keeping the other informed as to his own purpose and progress. Consensus demands communication."[6]

To properly fulfill the complete analysis of the term Community Education, we must also give scrutiny to the word *education.* Dictionary definitions tend to place education in a very structured, traditional setting of a combination of teaching and learning. Such a limited definition, however, does not display the potential of the term in bringing about change. A more relevant definition by H. G. Wells states that, "Education is the preparation of the individual for the community"[7], or by John Dewey, who defines education as, "that

---

[6] John Dewey, *Democracy and Education,* The Macmillan Co., New York, 1963, p. 26.

[7] H. G. Wells, *The Outline of History,* Garden City Publishing Co., Garden City, New York, 1929, p. 1089.

Community Education: What It Is and Is Not

reconstruction or reorganization of experience which adds to the meaning of experience, and which increases ability to direct the course of subsequent experience."[8]

It is from the conceptualization of community as a feeling rather than a geographical boundary and education as a means of understanding experiences and directing new ones that we may now proceed to a definition of the term, Community Education.

The defining of the term Community Education has been attempted by many persons over the years. It would seem logical that a proper definition might be developed by analyzing these many definitions and establishing a composite which represents a consensus of those who are experts in the field. In considering the many different definitions, however, one cannot give equal weight to each since some fall short of achieving a definition which includes the complete potential of the concept. For example, the National Association for Public School Adult Education limits its definition by focusing on the community school component of Community Education.

"When a school stays open in the morning, afternoon, and evening ... up to twelve months a year ... with programs geared to the needs of the total community which it serves ... for boys and girls, men and women ... involves representatives from the entire community in its policy formulation and its program planning – this is a community school."[9]

The problem with this definition is that it conveys the idea that Community Education is centered around programs in the school setting. In a similar way, the definition – adopted by the State of Michigan seems to place its emphasis on the school and its programs. It defines Community Education as: " ...... the composite of those services provided to the citizens of the community by the school district, excepting for those services provided through regular instructional activities for children aged 5 to 19 years. Such community school

---

[8] Dewey, *op. cit.*, pp. 5-6.

[9] National Association for Public School Adult Education, Washington D. C., "Community School Education – A Comprehensive Concept," Vol. XIV, No. 5, March, 1968, p. 3.

programs may include, among others, preschool activities for children and their parents, continuing and remedial education for adults, cultural enrichment and recreational activities for all citizens, and the use of school buildings by and technical services to community groups engaged in solving economic and social problems."[10]

While this definition tends to also imply that the regular school is not a proper part of Community Education, the often quoted definition by Elsie Clapp goes to the other extreme by equating Community Education with extensive interaction between regular school and its community. Miss Clapp states that Community Education is identified by the following characteristics:

"First of all, it meets as best it can, and with everyone's help, the urgent needs of people, for it holds that everything that affects the welfare of the children and their families is its concern. Where does school end and life outside begin? There is no distinction between them. A community school is a used place, a place used freely and informally for all the needs of living and learning. It is, in effect, the place where learning and living converge."[11]

In a similar fashion, other writers have arrived at definitions which are less than adequate for conveying the total concept. Consider the following:

"The school as an embryonic, typical community is one of the earliest forms of the community school concept. Its central feature is that the school, in all its internal aspects, should represent the kinds of human relationships and moral ideas that ought to characterize society."[12]

---

[10] Michigan State Board of Education, "Policies for the Distribution of Monies to School Districts for Community School Programs in 1969-70 in Accordance with the Provisions of Act 307, PA of 1969 (as adopted by the State Board of Education on October 1, 1969.)"

[11] Elsie Clapp, *Community Schools in Action,* The Viking Press, New York, 1939, p. 89.

[12] Othanel B. Smith, William O. Stanley, and Harland J. Shores, *Fundamentals of Curriculum Development,* Harcourt, Brace and World, Inc., New York, 1950, p. 535.

Community Education: What It Is and Is Not

"Any school is a community school to the extent that it seeks to realize some such objectives as the following: (a) educates youth by and for participation in the full range of basic life activities (human needs, areas of living, persistant problems, etc.); (b) seeks increasingly to democratize life in school and outside; (c) uses community resources in all aspects of its programs; (d) actively cooperates with other social agencies and groups in improving community life; (e) functions as a service center for youth and adult groups."[13]

"Community school is the term currently applied to a school that has two distinctive emphases — service to the entire community, not merely to the children of school age; and discovery, development, and use of the resources of the community as a part of the educational facilities of the school."[14]

It should be emphasized that these examples are not rejected as much for being inept as for providing a very limited perception of the scope of Community Education.

There are some definitions, which are felt to be more accurate in their attempt to clarify the meaning of Community Education and these are submitted as being more germaine to any discussion of the concept. While some of these appear to be more appropriate than others, they all contain the essence of true Community Education and are not stated here on any priority basis.

"Community Education is a process that concerns itself with everything that affects the well-being of all citizens within a given community. This definition extends the role of Community Education from one of the traditional concept of teaching children to one of identifying the needs, problems and wants of the community and then assisting in the development (or the identification) of facilities, programs, staff and leadership toward the end of improving the entire community."[15]

---

[13] Lloyd Allen Cook, "A Community School," *Encyclopedia of Educational Research,* First Edition, Macmillan Co., New York, 1941, p. 1002.

[14] Maurice F. Seay, "Two Distinctive Emphases," *Forty-Fourth Yearbook, Part I,* National Society for the Study of Education, University of Chicago Press, 1945, pp. 209-228.

[15] Hickey, *op. cit.,* pp. 31-32.

Community Education: From Program to Process

In April, 1968, the Board of Directors of the National Community School Education Association adopted the following definition for their organization: "Community School Education is a comprehensive and dynamic approach to public education. It is a philosophy that pervades all segments of education programming and directs the thrust of each of them toward the needs of the community. The community school serves as a catalytic agent by providing leadership to mobilize community resources to solve identified community problems. This marshalling of all forces in the community helps to bring about change as the school extends itself to all people."[16]

Still another definition is the following: "Community Education is an attempt to marshall all the educational resources within the community to create a laboratory for the management of human behavior . . . . Community Education is a theoretical construct — a way of viewing education in the community, a systematic way of looking at people and their problems . . . . It is based upon the premise that education can be made relevant to people's needs and that the people affected by education should be involved in decisions about the program. It assumes that education should have an impact upon the society it serves. It requires that all who are worthy of the name 'Community Educator' are involved in all facets of the community at large."[17]

In analyzing the differences in these definitions of Community Education, and in trying to look objectively at the characteristics of those which seem most complete and descriptive, the following ingredients seem to be necessary in developing a proper definition. The definition must include both the traditional and extended programs of education — for both children and adults. It must suggest impact on the entire community and stress community process as well as programs. Finally, it must project the catalytic role played by the school while recognizing the contributions of other groups and agencies. Taking all

---

[16] *Second Annual Directory of Membership,* National Community School Education Association, Flint, Michigan, 1969, p. 6.

[17] Donald C. Weaver, "Community Education — A Cultural Imperative," *The Community School and Its Administration,* Ford Press, Inc., Midland, Michigan, January, 1969.

Community Education: What It Is and Is Not

of these factors into consideration, the following definition is submitted in an effort to combine these many ingredients into one definition:

Community Education is a philosophical concept which serves the entire community by providing for all of the educational needs of all of its community members. It uses the local school to serve as the catalyst for bringing community resources to bear on community problems in an effort to develop a positive sense of community, improve community living, and develop the community process toward the end of self-actualization.

Objectives of Community Education

A philosophical presentation of Community Education is incomplete unless an attempt is made to describe the objectives that will hopefully be achieved. Since objectives are related to needs, it seems that before one can enumerate objectives, it is first necessary to examine the needs that mandate the development of Community Education.

One of the first of these needs for Community Education relates to the expanded educational needs of our society. The inadequacies of the current programs are apparent at several levels. They can be found in what might be termed the typical programs related to the K-12 educational offerings or in the needs for education by other groups in the community who are currently denied access to publicly supported educational programs.

In the case of the children in the community, one great need is in the area of early childhood education as it relates to preschool experiences. Most educators agree that in terms of both education and attitudes, the first few years of life have a tremendous impact on a youngster. Yet, few school districts provide educational programs prior to entrance into the traditional school at age five and in many states this does not occur until about age six. While federal programs have recently provided funds for encouraging such an educational opportunity to the community, there are still many districts which tolerate these programs as long as funding is available rather than view them as a responsibility of the school district.

For the child already in school, the need is one of relevancy — relevancy to the community in which he lives. Schools which were designed to meet the educational needs of the community, now frequently perform as though there was no community to be served. They have become institutions unto themselves which perform without regard to the students' environment or the influence which the community is having on the student. Schools continue to operate as though they represent 100 percent of the child's educational input despite the fact that the child is actually in school less than 11 percent of his yearly clock hours. There is a need for the school to be aware that the child is a product of his total environment and to be cognizant of the words by Dr. James Conant who said:

"The community and the school are inseparable. It has been established beyond any reasonable doubt that community and family background play a large role in determining scholastic aptitude and school achievement. Anyone who thinks they do not simply has not visited widely among American schools."[18]

For still another group in the community, there is a need for the traditional educational services of the schools. This group is the adult population — those persons who have passed the legal age at which they may avail themselves of the services of the public schools. Included in this group would be persons in need of basic educational skills, adults who need or want a high school diploma, persons who need vocational skills, and community members who desire other educational programs related to avocational interests, health, physical activity or personal problems. We have convinced our communities of the need for education, but in many instances are not providing such programs. Too often we proceed as though public education is a terminal thing despite our lip service to the concept that education is a lifetime process.

The second need for Community Education has developed as a result of our changing society. In the historical development of our country, it is easy to trace our community structure from one of small communities to large cities to that gargantuan society which we call the megalopolis.

---

[18] "The Community School — Past and Present," Editor, Clyde Campbell: *The Community School and Its Administration,* Ford Press, Inc., Midland, Michigan, December, 1963.

Community Education: What It Is and Is Not

To put this in perspective, we need to note the distinction made by the German sociologist, Ferdinand Tonnies. He described two kinds of culture, the gemeinschaft and the gesellschaft. The gemeinschaft is the type of community which is small and simple. It is characterized by:

A. A relationship between persons largely based on kinship

B. People who know most of their neighbors

C. Continuity brought on through informal controls

D. Little division of labor

E. A self-sufficient community

F. People with a strong sense of community identity

G. A general absence of special interest groups

In this type of culture, behavior is usually well-defined for all individuals. .

The gesellschaft is characterized by:

A. A community tie based on territory rather than kinship

B. Division of labor with great specialization

C. Proliferation of society and organization

D. Lack of acquaintance with others, even neighbors

E. Formalized social controls set by law and enforced by police

F. High interdependence with other communities

G. Anonymity of many persons, where few associate with community life.[19]

---

[19] American Association of School Administrators, "Todays Community," *Educational Administration in a Changing Community 1959 Yearbook,* National Education Association, Washington, D.C., 1959, pp. 35-53.

This type of society tends to foster a loss of sense of belonging, a loss of personal identity, a lack of concern for others, and creation of an environment which in many ways is abnormal for man. Thus, according to Tonnies, the old gemeinschaft community of our forefathers has disappeared, and in many communities the primary group has been disarranged.

"The result has been a considerable degree of cultural confusion. Most of us today may be likened to a traveler in a strange land where the crossroads are many, and the signboards few ... In short, the community, and especially the urban community, is no longer the highly integrative force it once was."[20]

With this kind of social change has come a number of social problems. One may question the idea of cause and effect, but there seems to be a strong indication that there is a direct relationship. These social problems include such things as a change in moral values, poverty, racial and social unrest, increased crime, dangerous increases in population, unemployment, lack of concern for our elderly, health problems, and the deterioration of our environment. These problems grow increasingly acute in our society and demand immediate attention in order to develop appropriate and timely solutions. While the inferences suggested may appear questionable, and the solution simplistic, it would seem logical that if these societal problems have been intensified with loss of a real sense of community, then the solution might lie in the recapturing of this feeling. And while it may be impossible to return to the gemeinschaft society, it may be possible to incorporate its strengths into our existing society by reorienting the existing social organization.

The third need for Community Education, and one closely allied with the second, is related to the failure of our existing social agencies. In the past, we have relied on traditional institutions such as the home, the church, and the school, to solve our social deficiencies.

---

[20] Newton Edwards, *The School and the Urban Community*, University of Chicago Press, Chicago, 1942, p. 196.

Community Education: What It Is and Is Not

"But these deficiencies are systematic, not local and specific, and specialized institutions seem unable to get at them. Our city homes have largely become places where we go to sleep. Our churches are centers of retreat from life. Our city schools are buildings where we study, not problems, but examples."[21]

The number of new agencies in our social setting has been increased over the years so that for every problem there is a multitude of social agencies designed to act upon it. A myriad of federal and state funded projects have also attempted to focus on our social needs. But these agencies, along with our traditional institutions, have failed to meet the increasing needs of our society.

The lack of coordination, the development of empire building, and the failure of our social agencies to perceive the real nature of the problems in other than a segmented fashion, have resulted in an inability to cope with the social issues. In fact, the school, the one institution on which we are predicting our greatest hope for change, is perhaps the institution that is most misdirected from its rightful role in society.

"Many schools are like little islands set apart from the mainland of life by a deep moat of convention and tradition. Across the moat there is a drawbridge, which is lowered at certain periods during the day in order that the part-time inhabitants may cross over to the island in the morning and back to the mainland at night. Why do these young people go out to the island? They go there in order to learn how to live on the mainland.

After the last inhabitant of the island has left in the early afternoon, the drawbridge is raised. Janitors clean up the island, and the lights go out . . . .

Such, in brief, is the relation of many American schools to many an American community."[22]

---

[21] Joseph K. Hart, *Social Frontier,* 3, December, 1936, pp. 73-75.

[22] William G. Carr, *Community Life in a Democracy,* National Congress of Parents and Teachers, 1942, p. 34.

Community Education: From Program to Process

With this as a background, let us look at the objectives of Community Education. Many writers have attempted to enumerate the things which typify Community Education. There are some differences in content and points of emphasis, based primarily on differing definitions. There are also, however, many similarities and the following is an effort to compile these general areas of agreement.

First, it is necessary to restate that Community Education is a philosophical concept and not a set of programs. This means that in the implementation of Community Education, programs become one of the devices in its development. The problem which arises is that it is difficult to refer to Community Education in operation without calling it a "Community Education Program." This dual use of the term *program* leads to misunderstandings and persons pursuing an interest in Community Education must maintain an awareness of this double usage of terms.

It should also be stated that Community Education is not the elimination of current educational endeavors in order to substitute something else. It is, instead, an expansion of the existing K-12 programs generally in progress. It may mean scrutiny of current curriculum practices to be sure that maximum effort is being made to have quality traditional programs and that these programs profit from the positive inputs of Community Education. The extended hours of the school, integration of educational services, addition of staff, and community involvement should serve to enhance the traditional program rather than harm it.

Let us now look at an enumeration of the objectives of Community Education. It should be noted that this compilation is an attempt to list the objectives in a general rather than a specific way and there is no attempt to put these objectives in any order of priority.

1. Community Education attempts to develop a number of community programs.

The term *program* here means specific activities aimed at community participation. The techniques for effectively accomplishing this will not be detailed here except to state that it is important that such programs be based on community needs and desires. These programs would include such things as adult education, high school completion, enrichment classes for school age students, avocational activities, vocational training, basic education, recreation, citizenship, cultural offerings, and special programs aimed at solving community problems. These programs will be an acknowledgment of the importance of developing a concept of education as a lifetime experience.

'We are going to replace the obsolete scholastic establishment of the past with a true educational system, a system which maintains only schools that are for all, young and old, true community schools."[23]

Certain precautions should be taken in the organization of programs. First, one must not lose sight of the traditional day program in planning other programs. An integration of effort should be made rather than the creation of a separate operation. Second, it is important to look at both individual needs and community needs. And, third, it is easy to fall into the trap of allowing all your energies to be used up in program development with the end result that a series of programs, serving a small portion of your population, becomes the total Community Education operation.

2. *Community Education attempts to promote interaction between school and community.*

This goal may be accomplished in the more overt and simplistic way of opening the school for more hours of the day, days of the weeks, and weeks of the year. Merely opening the school, however, does not insure the proper school and community relationship for making schools the relevant places they should be. The purpose of an improved relationship is to cause the traditional school programs to do those things for which they were intended — namely, to reflect the ideals of the society and to prepare young people for living in that society.

"A school that reflects the needs, interests, and highest educational and social ideals of its own immediate community (and the larger state, national and world communities of which it is a part) provides a better education, academically and socially, than the school which

---

[23] Hickey, *op. cit.,* p. 13.

stands apart. A public school is simply not doing an effective job unless the life of the school is integrated with the life of the community. Brief reference to a few of the basic principles of learning and curriculum construction, will make this clear.

A. Children learn best when they are interested in what they are doing; what better well-spring of interest can we find than the life and activities and environment in which the child himself lives.

B. Learning is most effective when there is a chance to experiment and find out and verify facts, individually and in groups; what better laboratory for identifying and solving problems than the community itself?

C. We must start in the learning process where the learner is now, building on these past experiences and devising new learning experiences; how can we know where he is now unless we know the environmental and experimental background the community has given each learner.

D. We must teach the whole child. Most of us would agree how is this anything but an easy platitude to which we give meaningless lip service, unless we can know the whole child in the light of his whole background?

E. The good modern school is the adaptable school: How can the school adapt to changes in the life of society unless the school is constantly being made sensitive and responsive to what goes on in the community?" [24]

The educational process must strive toward taking the students into the community and bringing the community into the school. We have drifted away from the purposes of education and our debate over the relative merits of book-centered and child-centered education has caused us to forget our responsibilities to education and its relation to the community.

---

[24] Kenneth H. Hansen, *Public Education in American Society,* Prentice-Hall, Inc., Englewood Cliffs, New Jersey, 1955, p. 260.

"The conventional belief... is that the young must be shielded from contact with the unpleasant and amoral aspects of the universe and that they must be kept in an ultra-conservative environment... the less the discontinuity between the life of the school and the life of the world outside, the better will be the training for life which the school gives to its students."[25]

It is from this need to identify with the community that schools can best provide for not only their particular students but also begin to develop information which can further expand the concept of Community Education as a total education program.

"As a result of their interest in the child and his total environment, school personnel initiate contacts with the community and consequently become aware of not only family-centered problems, but also other problems which hinder the community in its development as an ideal living center."[26]

From this concern for students and their problems there should develop an interaction with parents and techniques for bringing about community involvement. It is only through such techniques that education can become relevant and schools can play the role for which they were created.

3. Community Education attempts to survey community resources and to coordinate their interaction.

These resources will be both formal and informal, institutional and individual. In every community there are untapped resources of assistance which can be useful in both the traditional and Community Education programs. Industry and business have facilities, programs and activities which can be converted into educational aids and community assets. They are good sources for field trips, speakers, and teachers, and can often provide assistance, both political and financial, for community projects. In addition, the human resources in the community can

---

[25] Willard Waller, *The Sociology of Teaching,* John Witey & Sons, New York, 1932, pp. 33-35.

[26] Hickey, *op. cit.,* p. 34.

be of great help. There are many talents, professions and backgrounds in any community waiting to be utilized once they have been identified.

Such resources are not only of tremendous use to Community Education and its various programs, but by recognizing and using these resources another by-product accrues to the educational programs. For as community members are more involved in assisting in the educational and community programs, there is a personal satisfaction gained by those individuals who are involved and the result is often a more positive attitude toward the educational system and its personnel.

4. Community Education attempts to bring about a better relationship between social and governmental agencies.

In most communities, there are a myriad of agencies designed to cope with community needs. There are also many differing organizations and institutions which make up the environment of each community member.

"Bill Jones is in *Junior High School,* he goes to a *Sunday School*; has a home in a certain *neighborhood*; he is a member of a *scout troop* and frequents a certain *playground* from time to time; goes *camping* in the summer and attends *movies* twice a week. Those dealing with Bill in those different settings, know very little or nothing of each other."[27]

5. Community Education attempts to identify community problems and ferret out the needs of the community.

Ability to perform this function is dependent upon successful communication between the school and the community. It also implies a different role and responsibility for the school than the traditional teacher-pupil-subject role. If the communication channels are clear, then it becomes the responsibility of the school to assess the nature of the problem and decide what role it should play. It may refer, coordinate, or provide the entire service itself, depending upon the situation. The school is not all things to all people, but is instead an expediter, a facilitator or an ombudsman whose main concern is solving community problems.

---

[27] H. W. Hurt, "Relation of the School to Other Educative Forces in the Community," *Junior-Senior High School Clearing House,* 8, May, 1934, p. 526.

6. *Community Education attempts to develop a process by which the community can become self-actualized.*

The many problems which are plaguing our societies are compounded by the apathetic resignation of those who live within them. Action is dismissed by a feeling of powerlessness or by the attitude embodied in "you can't fight city hall." The solutions to problems and the changes required to improve our society can only be meaningful and long-lasting if such change comes from the community itself.

In Community Education, members of the community are made aware of the "community power" which they possess. They are shown how, by following a particular process in problem solving, they can cope with the needs of their community and bring about change. As they proceed, step by step, through cooperative ventures, they are able to recapture the feelings of involvement and a sense of community feeling which tends to motivate them toward further joint efforts with like-minded persons.

It is through this process that a community can develop real community identification and begin to solve community problems. And it is by this means that we can bring about the changes needed by our society.

"The traditional view of the school as an intellectual skill center cannot be expected to produce solutions to the critical problems which we face in this century. When viewed within the context of the modern social milieu .... the Community Education approach to problems can be viewed as a cultural imperative." [28]

---

[28] Weaver, *op. cit.*, p. 2.

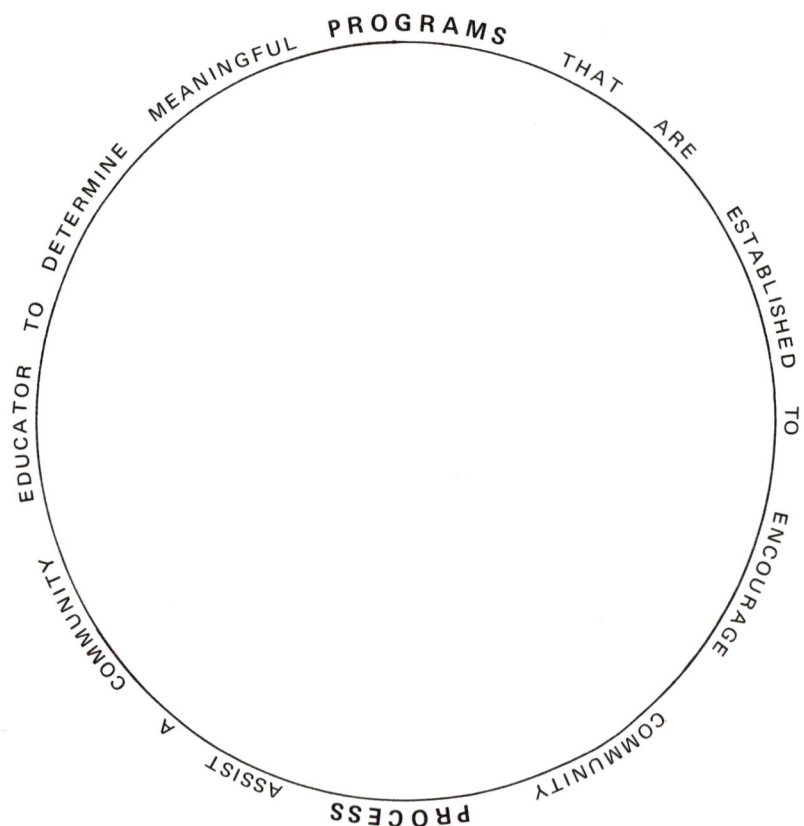

CHAPTER II

Moving From Program to Process

One of the topics most frequently debated by those involved with Community Education deals with the difference between *programs* and *process*. To many persons, the difference is not apparent because in many schools, Community Education and Community Education programs are identical.

To those persons who have a better grasp of the concept, however, there is a vital difference between the terms *program* and *process* and an understanding of this difference is critical to the development of meaningful Community Education. In fact, this difference is so important that without an awareness of the meaning and potential of each term, Community Education will probably not make the significant changes in the community of which it is capable of making. Therefore, let us first attempt to identify the differences between *programs* and *process* to which we have alluded, and then present a rationale and evolutionary context for the sequential development of each.

The misunderstanding related to the term Community Education program becomes more apparent when one realizes that the phrase is often used indiscriminately to describe different aspects of Community Education. On one hand, the term refers to overt activities of

Community Education: From Program to Process

participation by community members. Thus, adult education, roller skating, townhall meetings, recreation, and enrichment classes are Community Education programs. The term is also used, however, to describe the entire operation of Community Education in a community. Therefore, when a school district adopts the concept of Community Education and implements it into their community, they are described as having a Community Education program. Thus, the term has been used to describe the specific activities of Community Education as well as the total concept. For the purpose of this discussion, the term *program* will be used to describe specific activities. The term *process* will be used to deal with extensive community involvement and action.

The program aspect of Community Education will certainly meet many needs of the community. There are concerns in every community, however, which cannot be met by the program approach to Community Education. First, all people are not equally motivated to attend programs. Through timidity, suspicion, antagonism, unawareness, lethargy, or for other reasons, all community members will not attend programs which they may want or need. In fact, many times community members are not aware of those things which may be of most benefit to them, and often those most in need of services are least willing to avail themselves of existing opportunities. Therefore, programs at best will serve a small percentage of the total population.

Secondly, many people in the community have problems which are individual in nature. These problems are extremely difficult to identify and require different techniques to resolve. The solution of these problems will require a personal approach and the prescription for these problems may result in entrance into Community Education programs, a referral to existing social or governmental agencies, or an individualized solution designed by an appropriate person using available resources. This phase of Community Education is much more personal and might be construed as a particular kind of program.

Third, there are some basic assumptions related to Community Education which demand further development. These assumptions are:

A. Communities are capable of positive change.

B. Social problems have solutions.

C. One of the strongest forces for making change is community power.

D. Community members are desirous of improving their communities and are willing to contribute their energies toward such ends.

These assumptions relate to the ultimate goal of Community Education; the process aspect which results in self-actualization. The term community self-actualization is here used to mean the ability of a community to become the best that it is capable of becoming. In essence, community self-actualization is aimed at community development to the point that community members are involved in identifying problems and working through a process which enables them to plan courses of action and carry through on possible solutions.

If the assumptions listed above are true, communities are capable and willing to become self-actualized. The solution to the problems inherent in triggering this self-actualization is the organization and encouragement of community groups until they have achieved community identification, motivation, have mastered the techniques of a community approach to problem-solving; and have experienced success or failure with these techniques to the degree that they see the potential of their joint efforts.

When a community is capable of the initiative and sustained action necessary for attacking and solving its own problems, and when it is moving in the direction of the fulfillment of individual and community needs and community potential, then it can be said to be self-actualized.

With this as a background, let us now look at the evolutionary development of Community Education. There is no absolute best development formula, but there is impartial data available to indicate that an evolutionary step-by-step process is usually the way that Community Education begins and matures in a community.

The first step in the development of Community Education is the establishment of a general program. This happens for several reasons. First, the total concept of Community Education is difficult to grasp in its entirety. Any attempt to make an in-depth presentation on Community Education to persons unfamiliar with the term will often result in misunderstanding or rejection. The factors which seem to

Community Education: From Program to Process

immediately be most appealing and easiest to comprehend to the layman and uninitiated educator are the program aspect. Board members, administrators and community members are anxious to see their school buildings open, the lights on, and community members participating in an extensive variety of formalized activities.

The program aspect of Community Education will also be in two states. Initially, a set of programs is generally offered on the basis of what things have been successful in other communities. It must be kept in mind, however, that programs are meant to reflect the needs of the community and not assumed needs as perceived by the community school director. Therefore, either prior to the beginning of programs or soon after some initial programs are begun, it will be necessary, through surveys and personal contacts, to discover what programs the community wants and needs.

Once the program aspect is underway and dealing with at least some of the community's significant problems, it then becomes necessary to deal with some of the more personal problems. This phase of Community Education is much more time-consuming, much more difficult and, although more personally rewarding, success is much less apparent to those not directly involved. In order to successfully develop this aspect of Community Education, it now becomes necessary to have appropriate staff to service the community, an organizational structure in which to have two-way communication with the community, and the rapport necessary to such development.

The increase in staff will develop from increased responsibilities. In general, one person can usually organize and supervise formal programs in the community. To develop the personal, more individualized aspect of programs, however, it now is necessary to have a cadre of personnel, both paid and volunteer, large enough to contact and relate to all of the people in the community. This must be done while maintaining the staff needed to carry on those programs already begun.

The organizational structure may be developed in several ways, but must provide maximum opportunity for every community member to be aware of what is happening and to express his concerns in a way that will have impact on the proper people. This organization is sometimes achieved through block clubs in which communities are organized into block units and a person from that block represents his neighbors at community meetings. The organization is sometimes accomplished through the selection of representatives of organizations within the community to represent other community members. Other times the organization is accomplished through a sociogram technique in which community members identify those persons in whom they have the greatest confidence and with whom they have the most contact, and then those persons represent the community.

Whatever technique is used, the guiding principle should be to provide for maximum representation and involvement so that every opportunity is provided for; discovering those personal problems which need attention. As these problems are then identified, attempts are made to solve them. In many instances, the solutions are available through existing agencies or programs. In such cases, the individuals are given appropriate referrals and are assisted in making the proper contacts. In other cases, there will be no existing agency or program, and it then becomes the responsibility of the community director, with the assistance of other community members, to devise a means of dealing with the identified problem.

Attention should be directed, at this point, to the relationship between personal problems and existing programs. While programs were originally designed to service overt problems, they may also serve to originate a contact between the community school director and community members which could result in the identification of other more individual problems. These problems could then serve to generate new programs. In a like manner, as community problems are identified through the technique described above, new programs will be necessary to solve some of these problems. Once this sequence is begun, the proper relationship between problems and programs will be established, for the ultimate purpose of programs is to solve community problems. Programs based on problems are the only programs which have relevance to the community.

A few words should also be said about rapport. Personal problems are not shared with those who do not have your trust and confidence. While some problems are easily identifiable, deep-seated problems are only discovered when they are either subtly suggested or openly shared by those with the problem. It takes time and a particular personality to inspire the confidence necessary for this type of problem-discovery. However, it is only through such an accomplishment that the real problems of a community can be identified and dealt with.

Community Education: From Program to Process

The ultimate level of Community Education development is process. It is through this procedure that the latent forces of a community can be unleashed to cope with community problems and bring about change. In fact, while other levels of Community Education certainly improve community life, it is community process which holds the potential for the development of the true worth of Community Education.

To develop community process, we must return to a definition of community. To many people, *community* has come to be identified with a geographical area which remains static. The *community* to be worked with here, however, is largely centered around a feeling. The problem with most communities is that those things which identify it are boundary lines, formal names and governmental units. In community process, we are trying to re-establish a better community feeling based on the premise that there has been a loss of true community identity. We are seeking to help define a true community and move it toward the common good. We are trying to develop a sense of self-good among the members of a community which will lead to a sense of belonging; a community "esprit de corps," a sense of value of community and its potential for action. *Community* then becomes a feeling of relationship between those who have common problems, common interests and common goals. The problem becomes one of making the community members aware of these things and then showing them the advantage of working together. When successfully carried out, the bond of community becomes strong, as does the individual through his identification with others.

In selecting a community to work with, the person responsible for developing the process should recognize the value of the proper size of the group with which he is to work. There is no exact size for success, but in general, the area selected should be a primary group. By primary group, we are suggesting that it should be small enough so that many face-to-face interactions can take place and a great deal of personal contact is possible. It is generally recommended that the primary group should not be larger than three or four thousand people. This is usually the size of the population surrounding an elementary school and this is one of the reasons why the elementary building has been suggested as the basic unit for the development of Community Education. Even this size community might need some additional assistance to develop process but it is a workable unit.

Moving From Program to Process

There are also reasons other than size why the elementary unit has been designated as the basic unit of operation. First of all, there is a natural entree to the community through the children. Parents of elementary-age children are easily reached through their children, and even those in the community without children tend to be interested in helping youngsters. In addition, the location of the elementary building is usually strategic. Planners for most school systems plan elementary buildings to be most accessible to the children they serve, and in general they will be easily reached, often by walking by most members of the neighborhood. Elementary schools also represent a tax supported institution. As such, there is a feeling that they belong to the community. This public aspect of the school's existence often causes it to be the least threatening agency in a community to other agencies, and thus the one with the greatest possibility for community acceptance. The school building will also usually represent the finest facility in the community available for community programs and activities. One last factor relating to the value of the elementary school as the primary unit in Community Education is that the members of the community around an elementary building often have a great deal in common. While a secondary school will draw from a larger area and thus have a great deal of diversity, the people residing in an elementary area are more likely to represent a similar socio-economic group. As such, there will usually be many common factors in the nature of common problems, interests, perceptions and goals which will serve to enhance the identification of community.

Before process can begin, there are certain things which the person working with the community must ascertain about himself, and then attempt to develop between himself and the community. One of the first things is to analyze his own goals and motives. It is very easy for the director to establish himself as a leader and to try to achieve both political and personal power. He must be sure that his goal is the self-actualization of the community and not one of self-aggrandizement. He is also not a person who obtains his own desires by use of the power he has through community backing. Instead, his role is one of showing the community how, by working together through a certain process, they can attack and solve many of their own problems. If the director is successful, the group will develop no dependency on him and will often not recognize his total contribution nor his later absence from the group.

After examining his motives, the director is ready to move into the area of developing community rapport. It is important for him to realize the difference between rapport and acquaintance. Certainly, at the very beginning, the director should make every effort to make his community aware of who he is and what he does. This can be done through written communication and personal contact. Rapport with the community, however, is dependent on the development of trust and friendship and this can only be accomplished over a period of time. There are some who suggest that rapport can best be developed if the director is indigenous to the area he is serving and there are certainly many cases where this is true. There are also advantages to having directors from outside the community to be served. The outside director will be a stranger to the group and will have to make more adjustments in his behavior than an indigenous person will. He frequently will have more patience and sensitivity, however, and may be less threatening to the community. If a person is from outside the community he is serving and is having difficulty in gaining acceptance, he may turn to some community members to help him overcome this problem of relationship.

In any event, the development of rapport between the director and the community will depend upon his ability to develop trust and friendship. To do this, he must demonstrate trust and friendship himself. He need not share all the ideas and prejudices of the community, but must understand them. At first, the friendships will be one-sided with most of the effort being made by the director. To demonstrate his friendship he must be willing to share in the lives and experiences of the community. He can best do this by being as sincere as possible, accepting generosity when offered, and playing the role of the good listener.

Once rapport has been established and the community to be worked with is identified, the director is ready to begin the process. He is now ready to capitalize on the existing organizational structure that he has discovered or to develop structures where none previously existed. Using the representation of the community that most nearly provides for complete community representation, he can begin to involve community representatives in process. This beginning will demand a great deal of patience and certain human relations skills. He must constantly keep in mind that he is working on a process, not a formula, and that there will be many moments of disappointment. He

Moving From Program to Process

will discover from the initial contact that there are certain problems which he must tolerate until the group begins to develop some maturity and sophistication. He will soon find out that the group has a minimum sense of community and very little desire to become deeply involved. There will also be a sense of helplessness and a tendency to blame others for their problems. A great deal of the initial time will be spent discussing material things and the director might mistakenly get the feeling that people lack motivation for action and that they want no change.

During this period of time, the director will have a specific role to play. He should arrange for comfortable, relaxed quarters in which to meet and try to develop good internal relations within the group. He should build an atmosphere of tolerance for each other within the group, attempting to minimize stress and conflict and trying to get all of the group involved in the discussions. The director will also have to be aware of personal characteristics within the group and be attentive to the building of group cohesiveness. His frankness with the group members must be adapted to the maturity of the group. He should avoid emotional expressions and also avoid being self-righteous. He should check his own motives as well as those of the group and should constantly work at optimism while developing personal ability to accept disappointment. He must recognize and encourage ideas from the group and not stifle participation. The group will have some obvious shortcomings, but the director must realize that only group action is capable of developing community process. His role is to see group participants not as they are, but to see them for what they may become.

As the group begins to develop some internal relations and some sense of belonging it can now begin to work on the development of process. The first step is to identify problems for examination. These problems should be those felt to be pertinent to the community as identified by the members of the committee. It might be valuable to arrange these problems in a rank order based on perceived priority, but for the selection of the initial problem to be worked on, the group should start with a comparatively easy project. This provides a better opportunity for success and helps build proper habits for cooperation, assisting in establishing confidence in the process.

Community Education: From Program to Process

Once the problem is identified, the group then proceeds to the second step — discussion. The problem should be viewed from all possible perspectives and appropriate data concerning the problem should be collected in order to deal more adequately with it. All alternate solutions to the problem should be considered and the positive and negative consequences of each solution should be closely examined. The one best solution should then be selected.

During this part of the process, the director has specific roles to fulfill. The group may not be proceeding exactly as he would like. His main function is to keep discussions going, provide encouragement to the group, imply faith in their method of operation, and in general insist that the group keep working toward solutions, despite setbacks, without becoming overly dominant or directive.

The group is now ready for the third step — organization. They have decided on a possible solution and must now decide how to organize for action. Again, alternate methods are discussed. In some cases, writing a letter may be the best approach and the person is selected for that responsibility. In another, a committee may be needed and decisions are made about its membership and direction. In any event, the best pattern of organization is decided upon and the responsibilities for that organization are delegated.

The fourth step is action. The organizational phase is now ready to be implemented. This step involves the carrying out of that which has been decided. Those assigned this responsibility simply do the writing, the meeting, or follow through on any other technique designated by the group within the latitudes given by the group.

The fifth step is evaluation. The group now reassembles to discuss the process to this point. They look at the original goals to be accomplished, the technique to be used, and finally, the achievements in terms of the outcomes of their actions. They determine at this point their degree of success or failure.

The sixth and final step is continuation. This will be affected by analysis of the evaluation. If the degree of success is not what they had hoped, then they may return to any step in the process to reinstate their activities. They may decide to work at the problem through an alternate solution. In this case, they would start at step two and work

Moving From Program to Process

through the process again. They may decide to use the same suggested solution but organize in a different way. In this case, they would start at step three and follow the process from that point. They may decide that the failure was at the action level. They may decide that they have exhausted their abilities on that problem or that they have been successful, in which case they would start again at the beginning with a new problem.

The time required for this process may range from a few days to several months. While process has been described here in a rather simplistic way, it is complicated by many problems and disappointments. These will create internal struggles, personal conflicts, and a variety of emotional situations. It is important that the group establish ground rules which will help keep the group in operation during times of stress. It is also important that the group keep meeting and working to solve problems. Over-zealousness may be tolerated, but anti-social behavior or disassociation from the group should be prohibited alternatives from the beginning.

One cannot overemphasize the value of community process to Community Education. It is only at this level of operation, that true community involvement is achieved and true community identity and change possible. In addition, the process provides a technique whereby communities can deal with community problems. It provides a direction, a road map, a guide which when followed, allows a community to work systematically through a problem. Once the community has tried this process and becomes aware of its potential for solving community problems, it can then begin to feel the joy and community spirit which develops from a sense of community strength. Feelings of helplessness and impatience will begin to disappear and in its place a feeling for community and the power which it can generate will develop. As the process is repeated, communities will develop a sense of responsibility and sophistication which will result in better activities and better solutions. It is through this technique of community process that community self-actualization is achieved and the ultimate in the potential of Community Education is realized.

Community Education: From Program to Process

Developing Process
Community Problem Solving

    Identify Problems
        outgrowth of group discussion
        arrange on priority basis
        select problem to deal with
        establish goals to be accomplished

    Identify Solution
        consider alternate solutions
        consider good and bad consequences of each solution
        select most appropriate solution

    Organization for Action
        discuss alternatives
        select those to carry out action
        delegate responsibility necessary for action

    Carry out the Action
        implement the action suggested

    Evaluate the Action
        discuss outcome
        relate action to degree of success to continuation
        in case of success, return to beginning of process for a new problem
        in case of inadequate solution, return in process to most appropriate place

SECTION II

Initiating and Developing Community Education

CHAPTER III

Implementing the Concept

The development of Community Education is an evolutionary process which must begin and grow through the involvement of those to be affected by it. In fact, it would be a violation of the precepts of Community Education if it were developed in any other way. Community Education surmises that common problems can be identified and resolved through involvement of community members and that programs will develop from community needs. Both programs and process imply involvement, and it would certainly seem illogical to suppose that a concept proclaiming the need for community involvement should begin without such involvement at its inception. Community Education proclaims the belief that people should be done *with* and not *to* and this belief should be incorporated from the beginning.

Interest in Community Education may develop in many loci within the community. Since it is to operate through the school system, however, it is imperative that the board of education, as the governing body of the school district, be the object of the first efforts of those desiring to implement Community Education. Until the board is willing to make certain basic commitments to the support of Community Education, there is little to be gained and much to be lost by any attempt to coerce or by-pass the decision-making body within the school system.

Community Education: From Program to Process

The initial contact with the board of education will be primarily one of information giving, and this step will have to be repeated with all groups within the community. In such presentations, there is no set pattern for selection of participants. Presentations may be made to board members exclusively or to the board members plus representative groups of teachers, administrators and community members. In general, it has usually been found that community members are more readily receptive to the ideas embodied in Community Education, and board members consequently become more receptive when they are aware of the positive community acceptance of the concept.

At any rate, the first exposure should be a peripheral kind of presentation aimed at the overt advantages of opening schools and developing programs for community members. This presentation is intended to initiate the concept at an elementary level of understanding. The concept of Community Education is difficult to understand in its entirety. In addition, it is a dramatic philosophical change in educational belief. This combination of depth of conceptualization and change in traditional belief makes it almost mandatory that Community Education be introduced at the rate in which it can be absorbed rather than overwhelming the listeners in an initial contact and subsequently making them apprehensive about any commitment.

The initial presentation to the board will set the tone for future activities related to implementing Community Education. It may be that the board and others represented do not have an interest in the implementation of the concept. If this is true, then any additional efforts should be suspended until a time when interest is established. To proceed further would be self-defeating. Experience has shown that even when no obvious interest is demonstrated, the seed has often been planted, and may reappear at a later date.

Under no circumstances should the board of education decide unilaterally to begin Community Education. This type of arbitrary decision-making will only arouse suspicion and bring future problems to the program. The primary rule to follow is to move slowly and involve all those to be affected.

If the board is interested in pursuing Community Education, then several things should happen without any particular reference to sequence. Many additional exposures to Community Education should

Implementing the Concept

be made to the community and to the professional staff. School administrators must be made aware of the concept and its relation to their programs. Teachers must be exposed to this basic change in program and philosophy. Noncertificated staff must be made aware of what is going on, and community members must also be included in these introductory presentations on Community Education. The kind of presentations made to these groups must be similar to those first made to the board of education. Community Education should be presented and explained to the degree necessary and appropriate to the level of receptivity of the group. It will be the responsibility of those making the presentation to decide what this level should be. Again, let it be stated that no attempt is intended to defraud or disguise Community Education nor to claim it to be what it is not. It must be remembered that Community Education is a combination of programs and process comprised of student activities, use of buildings, adult activities, community service, community coordination, and community self-actualization. While the ultimate goal is to accomplish this in its entirety, it should be accomplished at the rate and to the degree to which the community is ready and able to assimilate it.

At the same time that the staff amd community are receiving this exposure, it becomes necessary to work more intensely with the chief administration and the board of education. If efforts toward Community Education are to proceed, it is important that key persons within the district be aware of the complete concept and the ultimate direction in which they are moving. This becomes necessary since there must be some assurance that at a later date there will not be a situation in which the development of Community Education is inhibited due to poor original communication with the chief decision-makers.

This intensive consultation should more thoroughly present the concept and its ramifications. School officials should be made aware of costs, financing, staffing and particularly the new role which the school is assuming in its community. Again, it should be restated that if at any point there is a reluctance to proceed, all efforts should be suspended until such time as there is a recognized need for Community Education within the district.

If there is at this point, however, a desire to continue, then it becomes necessary to work more in-depth with the community and staff. It is recommended that a committee be appointed for further study. This committee should include representatives of the faculty, noncertificated staff, students, lay community, churches, governmental agencies, social agencies, service groups, and any other community groups, formal or informal, who should be involved. This group should now be given a more thorough exposure to the concept and its implications. Every effort should be made to familiarize this group with theory and practice related to Community Education. Formal presentations, work sessions, study groups, and visitations are all ways of enhancing this group's knowledge of Community Education. The board of education should entrust this group with the complete exploration of this topic and charge them with the responsibility of recommending further action by the board of education.

The time involved in this total activity to this point will vary. It may take a few months and may stretch over a much longer period of time. While every effort should be made to keep things moving and avoid stagnation, it should be kept in mind that the most successful Community Education programs grow out of well-conceived plans developed by well-informed people. To be sufficiently well-informed to successfully plan an effective program will take time.

The Study Committee

The role of the study committee is a key one in the institution of Community Education. It is their responsibility to investigate the Community Education concept and make appropriate recommendations to the board of education. While the involvement and presentations to this point have been relatively cursory, the in-depth analysis now becomes the responsibility of this study committee. This group should be constantly aware of the fact that the future of Community Education in their community is highly dependent upon their efforts and that they have the responsibility of being fully informed and of recommending what direction their school district should take.

In selecting this committee, a few suggestions should be given. First of all, the committee must be representative of the community. Consideration should be given to the various groups within the community, organizations, governmental agencies, social groups and various community sub-divisions. Efforts should be made to include both the overt "power" structure and the less obvious leadership in the community. The selection of the membership of this group will greatly

Implementing the Concept

determine its future acceptance throughout the community — special attention should be given to selecting people who are truly representative of the community rather than simply selecting persons who occupy certain "traditional positions," but who do not reflect community thinking or exercise substantial community leadership. Proper leadership selection is described more completely in Chapter 4, "Organizing a Community for Process."

One other factor to be sought in this committee deals with potential out-put. Members of the group should be those who are dependable, ambitious and who have time to devote to the responsibility of the study. While certain people may be desirable, it is not beneficial to the final outcome to select people who do not have time to devote to this endeavor.

After the study group is selected, they should be given certain guidelines as to their function. The purpose of their efforts should be thoroughly explained to them. They should know the direction and the limitations of their function at the outset. This is to make certain that the group does not wander into some other area and assume a task for which they were not selected. The group should also understand that their task is to complete the study and make recommendations to the board of education. They should understand that the final decision belongs to the board of education and they should be prepared to receive either an acceptance or a rejection for their efforts. This preliminary clarification will keep them from misinterpreting their role and prepare them for the possibility of a negative board reaction. In addition, the group should be given a formal appointment by the board of education. This will give them a sense of both legitimacy and importance and start their activity on a positive note.

It is also wise at the beginning to set a temporary time schedule for the group. While this can be adjusted periodically, a time schedule tends to force the group to keep moving and places some degree of accountability on their time. The committee should also be made aware of a terminal date for their activities. Generally, the committee ceases to function at the time of their final report to the board of education. By terminating their services, they see an end to their responsibilities and the problems related to an indefinite appointment or an existing committee with nothing to do are eliminated.

Community Education: From Program to Process

In order to properly make their recommendations, there will be two things which the committee will have to do. First, it will have to know Community Education as well as is possible. This can be accomplished by reading extensively on the subject, visiting places which have Community Education, visiting with professors, administrators, teachers, city officials and citizens who know of Community Education, bringing experts into the community, and attending conferences, conventions, and workshops on Community Education.

The second thing which the committee will have to do is to become more familiar with their own community. As they become more familiar with the goals and purposes of Community Education, they will begin to perceive how it can be utilized to meet the needs and wants of their community. In order to properly recognize how well Community Education will operate in their community, it will be necessary to know what things need to be done. Pertinent information to be gathered will include such things as traditional educational needs of the community, avocational interests, vocational needs, recreational needs, community attitudes, existing agencies and programs, unmet needs of the community, and overall community spirit. It is often helpful to gather information on how the community perceives the schools and what changes the community would like to see made. It is also helpful to obtain information on the use of existing schools and other community facilities.

The committee should decide on whether Community Education is the direction their community should be moving, and if they feel that they should support the concept, then they must pull together a plan which they think would be most appropriate for the board of education to follow. One thing they should consider in their board proposal is the implementation of either a system-wide approach or an elementary school pilot project. The system-wide approach usually begins with the employment of one man for the entire system. This type of initial entry usually establishes a variety of program opportunities. The most that can legitimately be expected through this approach is to get lights on, buildings open, and programs in operation within the schools. While this approach does delay process for awhile, it does quickly get to overt programs that are highly visible and appealing to the board of education and the community. The developmental process from this approach would be in the direction of gradually moving toward building level directors as the programs increase and eventually employing persons to operate programs as the directors move into the community with "process."

The alternate way of beginning would be the "pilot project" approach. With this method, one or two buildings might be selected for full-time directors. If this technique is used, it is advisable to select those buildings to be used from both poor and affluent areas so as to eliminate stereotyping Community Education. This approach offers the advantage of getting to "process" much earlier. The director is now centered in a community of a workable size and can more quickly begin to demonstrate the advantages of community involvement and community interaction. The object of this approach is to show the growth that can occur in a particular community and thus cause other communities to request similar operations. The disadvantage is that on a system-wide basis, buildings will still continue to be closed, adult activities for the total community will be less available and the program will generally be less visible. This approach will be better for the individual community, but tends to receive less system-wide support.

The study committee should also include in its basic plan information on such things as staffing (full and part-time), financing, and a time schedule for implementation. The time schedule should provide for both the initial start and a projected timetable for the full implementation of Community Education.

The committee must maintain a firm belief in the value of making change slowly. Once the committee becomes an exponent of Community Education, there may be a desire on their part to immediately implement a total program. They must be constantly aware of the fact that their enthusiasm is based on information and experiences which the rest of the community does not have. A small start is often sufficient and all that the school system and the community is ready for. The committee must be cautioned to curb their enthusiasm to assure the accomplishment of long-range goals and purposes.

Reporting to the Board

Once the committee has completed its activities, it should report its findings and recommendations to the board of education. The future success of Community Education in that community is now dependent upon the action of the board. If the board is supportive, it is safe to

Community Education: From Program to Process

proceed with implementation, but if the board is negative or even "lukewarm" in their acceptance, more effort will have to be made to educate and convince the board of the necessity for Community Education in its district. The success of Community Education is so dependent upon board of education support that it would be a serious error to attempt to by-pass or develop Community Education without the board's backing.

If the board of education is supportive, there are certain steps which the board should take immediately to begin the implementation of Community Education. The accomplishment of these steps is not only necessary for the development of Community Education, but can determine the degree to which the board is willing to make a commitment.

The first action, and the easiest, will be for the board of education to formally resolve to support Community Education as a part of their basic belief in education. This resolution should officially declare the intention to make maximum use of school properties, provide for the educational needs of all the community members, and promote and encourage attempts to improve community life. The most important aspect of such a resolution is that it is understood by the board members who are making it. The implications of such a resolution are far-reaching and it is important that the decision-makers be aware of both the philosophical change and practical implications that such a resolution involves.

The second action should involve financial support. While it is likely that in its initial stages, Community Education will need some outside financial assistance, it is almost mandatory that some school funds be committed. This will eliminate the "something for nothing" attitude which may develop if there is no financial obligation. It is easy to tolerate almost any activity which is paid for by outside sources. The real test of commitment comes when one's own funds are involved. The ultimate goal is that Community Education will become an integral part of the total educational program and consequently be paid for through the same process as other legitimate expenses of the school system. The best way to assure the proper initial interest and continued support of Community Education is to establish financial support for at least part of the program from its beginning with an understanding that eventually the program will be completely supported through the school system. Without basic commitment to Community Education, which involves adequate financial support, Community Education will exist only as long as no effort is required from the school system, and operating in such a fashion will never become more than a peripheral program in the total school operation.

The third action of the board is to hire a trained community educator. Many times a school district will attempt to assign the duties related to Community Education as an extra assignment to someone already on the staff. The assignment of the task of director to someone already busy with other responsibilities often produces insignificant results due to time priorities and the level of importance assigned to the work involved. While there have been a few successful programs begun with part-time persons, it is generally advisable to start with a minimum of at least one full-time person. A full-time, trained person offers the best possibility for a good beginning. The right director, given time to accomplish his goals, is the most important factor in the success of the program.

Hiring a Director

The director of Community Education will be the key person in the future development of the program, and since, like most activities, the success is dependent upon the characteristics of the person involved, great care should be taken in the selection of the community school director.

There are certain identifiable personal traits which should be sought in the selection of a director. A good director should be a highly motivated individual who has a reputation for achieving his goals. He should be task-oriented so that his goals take precedence over his time. He should work well with people and be able to establish good rapport in a short period of time. He should be a good administrator, able to organize, execute, delegate, and plan. He should relate well to adult, youth and children. He should possess leadership characteristics which will make it possible for him to play both active and passive roles according to what is needed to bring the community into successful interaction.

A person with the above characteristics who is also experienced and trained is, of course, the ideal person for employment. It is not always possible, however, to find such a trained and experienced person. In such an instance, a person with the appropriate characteristics, should be identified and then provided appropriate training. Minimal training for such a person should consist of an intensive exposure to the Community Education concept and an internship with an experienced community school director.

Initial Task of the Director

The first responsibility of the community school director is to become familiar with the community with which he will be working. This familiarity will include at least two things — knowledge of the resources of the community and knowledge of the people who live within the community. Included in the things he should know are:

1. The history of the community — this would include information about the beginning of the community and its development. Of particular importance would be knowledge of the kinds of people who settled the area and the major influences which have affected growth.

2. Governmental organization — many communities are fractional parts of many different political units. It would be important to know what counties, townships, cities, villages, or other units are contained in the community to be served. It would also be helpful to know election procedures, inter-governmental relations, party organization, management type, and financial structure of those units. Of particular relevance would be the knowledge of how the school relates to these governments both financially and politically.

3. Business and industry — information should be obtained on the general activity of business, such as shopping centers and private enterprises, including the special organizations such as the Chamber of Commerce, which represents them. Major business and industrial developments should be noted with special attention to their economic contribution to the community.

4. Religion — information of value in this category would include the kinds and numbers of denominations and sects which represent the various segments of the population.

5. Education – not only would it be necessary to know about the public school system and the area it covers but other educational operations as well. This includes parochial and private schools, institutions of higher education and any other groups which engage in some type of education.

6. Agencies – information in this category would include any types of social agencies such as United Fund or government supported agencies which deal with particular problems such as unemployment, welfare, health, recreation, etc.

7. Communication systems – it would be necessary to know all the media sources such as radio, television, newspapers, and other publications.

8. Community members – it would also be necessary to know something about the people who live in the community. Collection of this data will help the director know more about the nature of the community and some of their needs. Information to be obtained should include such things as educational level, income, employment, family size, transiency, housing patterns, wants and needs.

In collecting such information about the community and its people, it should be recognized that the purpose is twofold. First, the director is trying to become as familiar as possible with the community he is trying to serve. Secondly, he is establishing a base of resources. The technique he employs in his operation should bring resources to bear on community problems. As he seeks this initial information about his community, he should constantly be soliciting information as to what services each of his contacts can provide the community. It is likely that there will be many offers and great willingness to aid community improvement efforts. It should also be stated that these resources will not only be agencies and organizations, but will also include individuals who will have both time and talent to offer their community.

The collection of this information appears as an awesome task and is indeed formidable. It is, however, a necessary one and there are some techniques which will make the task easier. Much information can be obtained from other groups which have already collected such information. This would include census information, data collected by public utilities, governmental studies, information available at libraries, information from historical studies, and studies done by other local groups and agencies. For the data which must be collected, two good sources of aid are student help and community volunteers. Student help is unfortunately often overlooked, but many directors have successfully used students to collect data and many have even claimed that such students have competency and eagerness beyond that of some adults they have used. The technique of using community volunteers has a double value. It gets the data collected and also produces participating community members with positive attitudes toward Community Education.

Developing an Advisory Council

A basic ingredient in the success of Community Education is the selection and functioning of an advisory council. There is probably no one council that can best serve all functions of a community, and it is important for the director to be well aware of different levels of councils and how they interrelate.

During the initial stages of establishing Community Education, it will be necessary to have a working committee to study the Community Education concept and to recommend to the board of education a plan for implementing Community Education into the community. This committee should be selected to be as representative as possible so that there is maximum input into the plan. Once the plan is formed and accepted, this committee will have done its job and should be dissolved.

The selection of advisory councils can now proceed from a grass roots base and should be created to provide necessary direction to the program. At the neighborhood level, there should be some type of neighborhood structure created which provides for maximum input from the community. A block type organization is one possibility. This allows each segment of 15 to 20 families to have a representative on a neighborhood council. These various block groups can select successive representatives so that it is possible to have a group at the local elementary school which has direct representative contact with each member of the community. The selection of this council can be made following the techniques described in Chapter 4.

Implementing the Concept

The goal being sought here is to provide two-way communication. The current direction of most communication is downward. Messages are directed to consumers and clientele with little or no opportunity for feedback except in extreme and hostile situations. By promoting a technique which allows all community members to voice their feelings and opinions to their block leaders, who in turn can pass this on to their representatives at the local elementary level, it is possible to make decisions based on community opinion and to be more aware of individual problems which exist in the community.

In a like manner, when the elementary neighborhoods are well-organized for communication, it now becomes possible to improve and expand the flow of communication to a much larger number of community members. This communication system can be enlarged to cover a junior high area, and, in turn, a high school area, and, finally, the entire community. The premise here is that the key to good communication and community involvement is a well-organized primary unit.

The organizational pattern suggested here is aimed primarily at providing improved communication, community involvement and identification of community problems. There will be a need also for involvement of decision-makers, agency groups, governmental leaders and the so-called "power structure." The difference in what usually happens and what is being suggested here is that most communities provide for advisory councils, made up of status leaders who advise on community problems, set priorities for these problems, and frequently decide on the course of action to be taken in solving them. This procedure tends to be perceived, even if well intentioned, as "doing to" certain people. The technique being offered here suggests that problems and priorities will be decided at a neighborhood level and that these neighborhoods will also be represented at all levels of decision-making so that their perception becomes one of being "done with."

Starting with Peripheral Programs

While the program aspect of Community Education is not the ultimate goal, it is often the best method by which to proceed. First of all, programs can be understood and are most appropriate in the early stages of Community Education. They do provide for the needs of

Community Education: From Program to Process

certain segments of the community and while they may serve only a small portion of the community members, beneficial services are being provided that were not available before.

In addition, programs will tend to get the buildings open and the lights on. Initially, this will meet most expectations held by the school board, staff, and community. In-depth understanding of Community Education requires an abstraction which takes time to conceptualize, but most of those exposed to Community Education will see the need for programs and activities. By starting classes and programs of various kinds for various age levels, there will be an immediate satisfaction and approval by school and community, and this will provide the atmosphere for future positive expansion of Community Education.

There has been much discussion about how these first programs should be selected and how much surveying is necessary before such activities should start. It would seem that such programs should reflect community wants. It is important to explain, however, that we are talking about initial programs which are general in nature and cursory at best. At this point, any extravagant attempt at basing these programs on community need would consume more time than would be warranted. This is not to deny that eventually all programs should reflect wants and needs, as shall be pointed out later, but during this stage of development, a satisfactory program can be developed by the director. This is also not to imply that no community suggestions should be used. Certainly if there is evidence that community members want a specific program, it should be offered. It has been found, however, that when programs are first started, there are certain ones which will be successful and others that can only be instituted at a later date when time allows for the effort needed to make them succeed. By checking with other community school directors it is possible to find those programs which will most likely be successful in this initial stage. Spending time having community members select programs will only substantiate what is already known and result in an unnecessary expenditure of time and energy. There are many who will be affronted by this suggestion, but the affront will usually represent their lack of experience in Community Education or an excessive desire to demonstrate their democratic idealism.

Implementing the Concept

Making Programs Reflect Community Needs

Once programs are operating and buildings are open, it now becomes necessary to consider making the program relevant to more of the community needs. The procedure described so far will serve to create a public image and deal with the most obvious community needs. Discovering other needs and developing programs to resolve them now takes a greater investment of time. The goal becomes one of finding techniques to assure future programs based on what community members want and need.

Part of this can be accomplished by soliciting information from those already in the programs. Either by survey or personal contact, it will be possible to get some feeling for what should be continued and what should be added. This information will be valuable since those responding are already participating and can provide some insight into executing programs. The disadvantage is that continuing to build programs by this method alone will cause future programs to reflect only the wishes of the small percentage of the community already involved.

Another technique, then, which may be used is the community survey. This method provides an opportunity for input from each community member. The survey form may include suggestions for program offerings with an opportunity for writing in other suggestions. Other information regarding possible times, dates, and costs may also be collected. There are some problems inherent in this type of survey. It will take time and manpower to collect such information. There may also be a cost factor involved. Surveys can be sent home with students but this leaves out the large percentage of people who do not have children in school. Mailing is a possibility but this requires an address list, addressing the mailings, and the cost of postage. This also raises the problem of return. Even with return, self-addressed envelopes, the percentage of return will be relatively low.

The best survey technique is probably a door-to-door survey. This method assures a high rate of return and the advantages of face-to-face contact which will accommodate responses not provided through a written return form. The biggest problem presented, if this technique is to be utilized, is finding appropriate manpower to accomplish the task.

Another excellent means of collecting such information is through advisory councils. The use of this method assumes that those on the council are truly representative of the community. This method does offer the advantage of input from community leadership as well as from people who represent concerns of governmental units, agencies, and institutions within the community.

Probably the best technique is a combination of some or all of the preceding methods. It should be pointed out that whichever method is used, the responses will still reflect the opinions of only a portion of the population, and that there will be quite a discrepancy between the number surveyed and the number who participate in the final programs. This is due to the fact that it takes a definite effort to find out what people want and need, but it takes a different kind of effort to get people to do those things which will improve or change their condition, even when appropriate programs are offered.

Expanding Community Education

As indicated previously, Community Education may begin either on a system-wide level (with one person serving the entire community) or on a pilot type program starting with one or more smaller units such as an elementary school area. In the beginning, when programs are starting to develop, the initial staffing is probably sufficient. As Community Education starts to mature, however, it will become important that additional staff needs be met. In fact, the most frequent hindrance to the development of Community Education is the plateauing of the program, generally as the result of failure to add staff at appropriate times.

The program aspect will grow rapidly. The number of classes and activities will increase and more and more demands will be made upon the time of the director. He will soon find that surveying the community, organizing programs, advertising, staffing, registering, supervising, financing and administering programs will take all of his time and that regardless of his energy and commitment, he will be unable to expand his activities. It is at this point that the commitment of the decision-makers in the school district is most important. For only by adding staff will any expansion be possible.

Implementing the Concept

One of the immediate needs will be for additional staff to expand programs. As more and more buildings develop programs, it becomes necessary to have more administrative assistance. The program aspect is not the only concern, however. If Community Education is to reach its potential, more emphasis will have to be placed on other dimensions of Community Education. Coordination of all governmental and social agencies is an important part of Community Education. This is a time-consuming responsibility which takes a certain kind of leadership and subtleness which cannot be effectively achieved if there is not time to devote to this endeavor. In addition, Community Education is premised on community involvement, and this can only be achieved by having at least one community school director in each segment of the community, comparable to an elementary school unit, with enough time and staff to effectively permit him to know and work with his community.

Moving to Process

It may seem redundant to repeat those aspects of Community Education which relate to involvement and process. They are so crucial, however, that they will be repeated so that the point can be emphatically underscored. The ultimate value of Community Education lies in its ability to bring about change and subsequently resolve community problems. This idea is based on the belief that communities can and will tackle their own problems if they are assured that there is the possibility that such an effort might succeed. The belief is that true democratic process if founded on representative government which decides issues on the basis of what is good for the community and that in order for it to function effectively, there must be input from all segments of the community. The error in this logic is that there has been no organization of, nor opportunity for, community groups to interact and develop their community attitudes, and, as a result, they have come to feel quite powerless and disillusioned with the system.

The development of the local organization needed will take a great deal of effort by the community school director. He will need to organize his small elementary community (about 3,000 people) in a fashion in which a representative group can interact, keeping in mind the fact that they represent their community members and must constantly strive for input from those whom they represent.

Community Education: From Program to Process

This type of development is the hub of Community Education and the ultimate in achievement. It takes many years to reach this level of community involvement and boards of education must be aware that this difficult step is only accomplished by the addition of appropriate staff to do the job.

This, however, is what Community Education is all about and it is the level to which all communities should aspire. To settle for less than this is to fractionate the concept of Community Education and to deny your community those parts of Community Education which can really make the difference in community life.

CHAPTER IV

Organizing a Community for Process

The preceding pages have established a conceptual difference between Community Education programs and Community Education process. Let us now turn to the techniques for organizing a community for growth and the establishment of procedures for achieving citizen involvement. While the techniques that are presented are not the only ones available to gain community process, they do seem to incorporate many of the generally accepted ideas for process held by a variety of community educators, sociologists, and others concerned with community development.

It seems clear from the preceding pages that one of the ingredients crucial to achieving community process is organization. Unless a community is somehow structured to achieve pre-established goals, its efforts will often be at cross-purposes and therefore self-defeating.

It is necessary to establish some type of system which assures four basic processes:

1. Adequate communication between citizens and community institutions.

2. A problem-solving process that assures a relationship between program planning and existing community problems.

3. A coordinated and comprehensive planning effort that assures recognition of the needs and concerns of all segments of the community.

4. A means of evaluating the effectiveness or noneffectiveness of programs designed to assist a community.

Without each of these four elements, a community cannot reach its maximum potential, and the quality of life that is possible within a given community will not be as great as it could be.

The educational system seems to be the logical institution to initiate a well-defined, well-developed community organization. The public schools possess a variety of advantages. Each public school system has publicly owned facilities in each neighborhood. These facilities incorporate a variety of meeting rooms, audio-visual equipment, duplicating processes, and human talent that is required in any attempt to organize a community. The public school is viewed by the general public as nonpolitical. It is designed to serve the total community rather than special interest groups. Because of this, it is (or should be) an unbiased objective base for establishing a structure to serve the entire community.

By its very nature the public school presents a unique combination of community thinking and life; a combination of all aspects of American society not found in any other existing institution. It reflects not only the basic elements within the community, but also the very best that the community can achieve. It is a combination of the practical day-to-day life of the community and all of the hopes and aspirations the community has for its future, both individually and collectively.

The importance of the need for the public school system to accept a broader responsibility of its role to include the entire community is expressed by Kenneth Hansen:

> "A school that reflects the needs, interests, and highest educational and social ideals of its own immediate community (and the larger state, national and world communities of which it is a part) provides a better education, academically and socially, than the

school that stands apart. A public school is simply not doing an effective job unless the life of the school is integrated with the life of the community."[1]

This same sentiment is also expressed by Brunner and Hallenbeck when they state:

"It is equally important to recognize that everyone has a stake in the improvement of his community. To attempt to build up the strength and influence of a local business or institution irrespective of what happens to the community over time, may gain an initial measure of success, but is self-defeating in the long run. What is true of schools is almost certainly true of other institutions. It will be recalled that community factors were about twice as powerful as educational factors in determining what the school was like. For an institution to progress beyond relatively narrow limits, therefore, the community itself must also progress." [2]

It is becoming increasingly evident that schools must initiate a more positive and active leadership role in the community, not only because of the unique nature of public education in this country which provides an opportunity to greatly assist in community growth, but also because it makes good sense educationally to become involved in the community's problems. The growth of the educational institution and the growth of the community as a whole are intertwined.

If the schools are to accept their proper leadership roles within the community, and begin to work toward a community organizational structure as a goal for achieving community process, what must be done to get started?

To begin, it is imperative to know exactly what the community is and what variables exist within it that directly effect its progress and growth. The acquisition of this knowledge requires a fairly sophisticated assessment of the community and a basic understanding of

---

[1] Kenneth Hansen, *Public Education in American Society*, Prentice-Hall, Inc., Englewood Cliffs, N. J., 1955, p. 260.

[2] Edmund de S. Brunner and Wilbur C. Hallenbeck, *American Society and Urban and Rural Patterns*, Harper & Row Bros., New York, 1955.

community structure and organization. This assessment stage is often ignored, or at best done poorly and given rather limited attention and consideration. The present lack of attention given community assessment does not indicate an acceptance of its unimportance, but rather a lack of understanding regarding the whole process. In fact, the importance of assessment in community development and organization is essential if we are to believe Nelson, Ramsey, and Verner in their book, *Community Structure and Change:* "Social change is not introduced in a vacuum but in a structure of human relationships, a veritable network of subtle and yet undeniable forces operating to maintain the status quo. Without a thorough assessment of these dimensions and elements, the success of a community development program is left to chance and probably doomed to failure."[3]

Most community assessment done by educators (when it is done at all) is an analysis of a summation of a variety of statistical data usually gathered through some type of survey or collection of surveys. Information, for example, is collected on economic levels of community members; church affiliation; educational levels; community size; age, race, and sex of the population; population growth and density factors; and a host of other facts about the community. There is no question that information of this type is valuable and assists in understanding the community to be served. To accept only data of this type, or to assess only rather cold factual statistical aspects of human beings is a mistake. Good community assessment must also recognize that the communities share certain beliefs and values and mutually hold certain aspirations, concerns and community goals. To ignore the subjective "feeling" aspect of a community when attempting to assess it, parallels an attempt by a medical student to establish the basic determinant of life by studying only a cadaver. Human beings are more than a combination of factual data; and communities, because they are composed of humans, require more than an overview of easily collectable facts if meaningful assessment is to occur.

---

[3] Larry Nelson, Charles Ramsey, Coolie Verner, *Community Structure and Change,* The Macmillan Company, New York, 1960, pp. 403-404.

Organizing a Community for Process

To appraise or diagnose a community by utilizing information beyond what is normally collected, to determine to what extent goals of the community are being achieved, and to determine what might be done to further the attainment of these goals, requires a response to a variety of questions, such as:

1. Is there a set of common understandings, goals, beliefs, and values held by the community?

2. Is there unity within the community that allows it to function at an acceptable level?

3. Is there a tendency for large sub-groups to develop with opposing purposes, causing conflict and tension with the community?

4. Are the institutions within the community (churches, schools, government agencies, etc.) viewed as positive community forces or as burdens to the taxpayer?

5. Do people have an opportunity to confront their problems as a group and solve them?

6. Do barriers exist that reduce opportunities for people to become actively engaged in working for social change, community change and institutional change?

Considering questions of this nature assists the community educator in establishing a "feeling level" for the community under study. This, in turn, opens a whole new dimension of understanding.

Assessment of this type is not easily made by a survey or analytical study. People do not respond to a question involving values or personal concerns as easily as they do to a question concerning age, sex, or number of cars in the family. Because this is true, different techniques must be utilized. The method that will be suggested in this chapter is only one of many possible methods. It is described in detail because it not only provides a means of collecting information beyond the factual, easily collectable data that is usually used, but because it also provides a means for community involvement and community development.

Organizing a Community
(One Approach)

To initiate our discussion on the organization of a community, it is necessary to begin with several assumptions. Rejection of any one of the assumptions invalidates the organizational structure being presented.

Assumption No. 1

It is impossible to involve all people in any meaningful community organization. Some form of representation must be established. The size and complexity of our society and existing communities negates the possibility of involving all people in discussion and dialogue in a process of community problem-solving.

Assumption No. 2

There is a direct relationship between community leadership and a knowledge and understanding of community problems and needs. True leaders (those who are perceived as leaders because of personal qualities rather than status position) are ascribed leadership positions because they understand, accept, and cope with the problems of life and of the community. An individual's ability to understand and assist in the solution of another's problem is an integral part of leadership.

Assumption No. 3

Most communities are a composite of many segments (both formal and informal) and by determining what segments exist in a community and finding the leadership that exists within these segments, it is possible to establish a cross section of community thinking and concern. Because real leaders do understand and reflect the attitudes and feelings of those ascribing them a leadership status, they can represent these attitudes and feelings with a fair degree of accuracy. Leadership is not authority, since true leaders are more bound by the group policy than the other members.

Assumption No. 4

There are basically two forms of leadership, formal and informal, and both must be recognized and incorporated into any meaningful community organizational structure. Formal leadership exists within the organized structure of the community. It includes business and industrial leaders, governmental officials, and other leaders emerging from the formal, organized, structure of the community. This group represents the traditional community leadership, as identified by Floyd Hunter.[4]

A number of informal structures also exist within a community with their own leadership structure. The informal nature of these organizations makes them no less important. Unlike the pyramid structure of leadership described by Hunter, the informal structure appears in a parallel pattern. Important community issues, ethnic and religious concerns, and other special interests create groups with a fairly narrow scope of interest, but with a definite, although somewhat informal, leadership structure within them. These parallel structures, while maintaining a variety of goals and purposes, often incorporate many of the major community issues.

To ignore the formal leadership structure is to ignore the wealth, traditional community power sources and vast majority of the citizenry in the community. To ignore the informal structure is to ignore the voices for change; the alienated, the concerned, and the minorities.

Assumption No. 5

Once formal and informal leadership has been found, it can be used as a communication bridge between community institutions and the general public. This is true because of the unique rapport that exists between genuine leaders and those ascribing leadership.

---

[4] Floyd Hunter, *Community Power Structure,* Doubleday and Company, Garden City, New York, 1953.

TRADITIONAL FORMAL STRUCTURE [5]

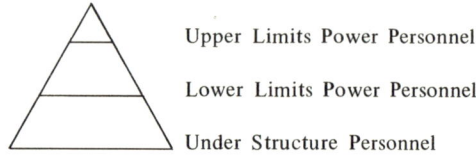

PARALLEL INFORMAL LEADERSHIP STRUCTURE

COMBINED FORMAL AND INFORMAL LEADERSHIP STRUCTURE

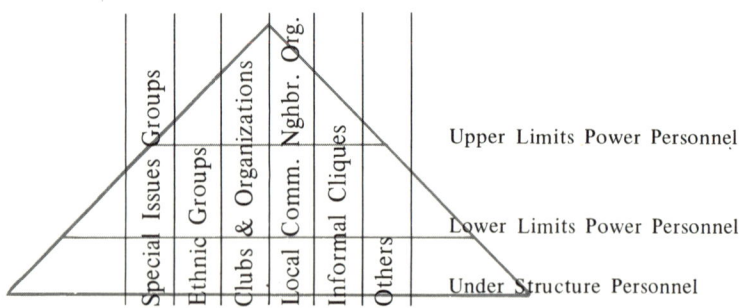

---

[5] Ibid, p.95.

Organizing a Community for Process

From the five assumptions presented, it is suggested that one of the best means of assessing and describing community needs and problems is through determination of formal and informal community leadership and that that leadership, because of its unique relationship with the community, can provide the basis for an excellent two-way communication process between community institutions and their constituency.

Determining Community Leadership

With the acceptance of the five assumptions previously listed, it is now possible to initiate a discussion regarding the determination of existing community leadership. While a variety of excellent techniques exist, one that seems to allow for the determination of community leadership while assuring appropriate representation from many diverse community groups is a modified version of a plan presented by George Brower resulting from a discussion between he and Irwin T. Sanders. This plan is initiated by interviewing public figures from as many segments of the community as can be determined, including government, business, banking, industry, social services, and health.

During this interview, questions similar to the following should be considered. Questions one and two should be used and either questions three or four.

1. · If you had a plan for improving some part of the community that needed total community support, who would you go to to seek support? Name five and list the part of the community that each represents.

2. In your estimation, who are the five most successful people in the community? List the part of the community that they represent.

3. If you wanted the thinking of the total community on an important issue, what five people could best represent the community? List the part of the community that they represent.

4. If your community was involved with other communities on a regional plan to restructure community services for the entire region, who would you select as representatives from your

community? Name and list the part of the community they represent.

The individuals mentioned should then be asked the same questions. The process should be repeated until the names begin to be repetitious. At this point, the data collected should be analyzed, both for frequency of mention and for cross-area representation.

There are only two modifications that are suggested to this plan.

1. Unless careful consideration is given to the initial determination of community segments, only the formal leadership structure will be included. It is necessary to identify the parallel leadership structure as well as the formal. Informal leadership within ethnic groups, neighborhoods, special interest groups, etc., must be identified if true representation of the community is to result. This can only be accomplished at the inception of the study by recognizing the informal structure of these community segments, incorporating them into the study, and attempting to find the leaders of these groups.

2. By adding two questions to the four suggested, extensive additional insight can be gained about the feelings of the community.

    a. What are the three most important problems facing the community?

    b. What are the major strengths within the community that can be utilized in combating the problems mentioned?

These two questions can provide insight into community concerns and potential resources for the solution of these concerns.

In analyzing the leadership list it is important to not only find individuals that are mentioned frequently as leaders, but also people who seem to be mentioned frequently by diverse elements within the community.

While the process works best on a community-wide basis, it can also work effectively on a local neighborhood basis. By identifying community segments in a local neighborhood and using the same procedures, neighborhood leaders can be identified. Because homes within an elementary school boundary often do not form a natural community, community leadership does not always fall within the boundaries of the elementary school. Provisions for the inclusion of community representatives from outside the elementary school boundaries must be made. The process described establishes leadership in a community. The inclusion of interested individuals not selected as leaders is also important. The process suggested, when used at a neighborhood level, will provide names of leaders in the community. Many leaders will not be pinpointed and provisions should be made for their inclusion in any determination of leaders. It is at this point that the community school director must rely upon his own intuition and knowledge of his service area. If he has been working with a block club, a P T A, a merchant's group, etc., and knows that there are individuals within the groups that are leaders, they should be included in a leadership listing, regardless of whether or not their names are specifically mentioned in a study. What we are recognizing here is the value of a systematic community study, but also recognizing the limitations that exist. No community study techniques presently exist that are completely accurate and inclusive.

Once data has been collected, on either a community-wide or neighborhood basis, a priority list of community leadership can be established that incorporates the various leaders of different community elements within the priority structure. Establishing who the leaders in a community are provides the basis for establishing the problem-solving process for the community—the community council.

Establishing a Community Council

It seems evident at this juncture that the establishment of an effective community council should be based upon the priority listing of community leaders that results from the community leadership study. Establishing a council of 15-25 people based upon the pre-established leadership listing of the community provides a microcosm of community thinking and an opportunity for extensive two-way communication with the entire community. Obtaining individual leader's consent, then, is essential. This is often difficult because school committees have frequently been misused in the past and few citizens are willing to expend time and effort with committees they consider meaningless, whose function is not clear, and whose conclusions and suggestions are often ignored. The purposes of the community council, then, must be carefully determined prior to asking any individual to serve. The educational system must also analyze its own motives for establishing a council, honestly answering whether or not their purpose in establishing a community council is for honest communication and feedback or for support of educational programs that are endorsed by the existing administration. It is important to ascribe a clear and concise role to any citizen's group at its inception and to assure that group that the time spent will be on important community and educational issues and problems. Let us look at existing concepts of a community council for a moment and define what it is, or should be, and what it is not.

Many community councils are misused and, in fact, misnamed. They are often composed of a group of people chosen arbitrarily with little forethought as to total group composition or purpose. The members are called together occasionally, often to discuss rather meaningless aspects of the Community Education program. The statement is frequently made, for example, that the community should assist in planning the program that is provided for the community. In response to this, the community school director establishes a citizen's group to vote on the course offerings that will be presented the following semester. We maintain that this is not an appropriate use of a community council and is, in fact, a misuse of it. It is really an attempt to maintain minimal community involvement—involvement at a safe level—so that the community school director or the educational system can establish the real priorities and make the major decisions.

Community councils made up of true representatives of the community can be of invaluable assistance in establishing educational purposes, providing an awareness of community problems and concerns, and assisting in establishing the basis for programs that might help solve some of these problems. A community council should be issue-based, rather than program-oriented. It should assist the educator in clearly understanding community thinking and concerns. It should be a communication bridge between the many diverse and opposing groups in a community, assuring two-way communication between school and community.

Good community councils incorporate several general concepts:

1. Adequate representation from all segments of the community. Any decision-making process should incorporate the thinking of the community in it, regardless of the time and effort required to assure this.

2. An opportunity for the community, through its representatives, to present its concerns and criticisms to educators in an open and positive setting.

3. An opportunity for an interchange of ideas. When community problems are presented to the educator for consideration by the educational establishment, an opportunity should be provided the educator to present his concerns to community leaders for feedback into the entire community. The council should assure a process of give and take; an opportunity for discussion of issues and points of view.

4. Establishment and support of strong community leadership. This is an essential part of community growth and should be encouraged whenever possible. Community councils should greatly strengthen and encourage existing informal leadership by providing opportunities to accept leadership responsibilities.

5. Positive and cooperative efforts between existing public and private agencies designed to serve the public interest. These should be considered an essential product of any good community council's efforts. As councils become involved in discussions of community problems and concerns, much of the discussion will extend into areas of concern outside of the responsibilities of education. This presents an excellent opportunity for involving other community agencies in the solution of problems of mutual concern.

It appears that there is very little relationship between these five general concepts and many of the existing councils. The five principles established here seem to indicate that community councils must become problem-solving groups. Councils provide the opportunity to combine the thinking of educational and community leaders, and direct it toward solving important community problems.

The authors believe that there are specific sequential steps that a community council should take in attempting to become a meaningful problem-solving group.

First, some agreement must be reached concerning which problems facing the community are the most crucial. This can only be done through extensive discussion and debate. Once the problems have been established, they should be listed by priority—the most important problems first. This again takes extensive discussion. It is important to recognize that the very nature of a representative council will dictate a great deal of conflict within the group during these initial stages. All of the conflicting interests and goals of the community have been compressed into one small group called a community council.

Once problems have been determined and assigned priorities, the next question becomes that of determining the best way to attack them. This can be done by taking each problem that has been identified and agreed upon and dissecting it into smaller parts, attempting to discover major causes for each problem. Once these causes are established, the group should then attempt to determine general objectives that should be accomplished by any program designed to solve the problem. Some objectives might be established that will require total elimination of the problem, others that might require a greater understanding between people, and still others that attempt to merely begin to attack the problem. Establishing objectives, whatever they are, establishes the general direction that must be taken by any program that is designed to solve a given problem.

Once problems have been determined and objectives established, the actual problem-solving process can begin. The next step obviously becomes that of asking what can be done. The resources of the entire community should be considered when answering this question, not just those of the education system. Initiation of this stage is best handled through several brain-storming sessions. The group should be encouraged to verbalize as many ideas as possible, attempting to obtain a variety of different suggestions for solving or viewing the specific problem being discussed. Once this has been done, the group should expand upon the variety of ideas presented, weighing the potential advantages of each suggestion against other suggestions, discussing possible outcomes resulting from each approach, and determining relationships between the approach suggested and the pre-established objectives that the group wanted to reach. This process will ultimately result in some rather specific means of dealing with specific community problems.

Solutions will usually require the combined efforts of many agencies, community groups, and the schools. Once this point is reached, it becomes the community educator's task to work through the council and establish a means of responding to the suggested solutions. This action phase may be assigned to any members of the committee or the director himself, depending upon the nature of the action and the person or group most appropriate to respond. Because a variety of agencies have usually been incorporated into plans for solving problems an ideal opportunity is presented for getting different community agencies together to establish cooperative programs. If there is a limitation in funding (and there usually is) the problems at the top of the priority list should obviously receive the greatest amount of available resources. By combining the resources of many agencies, you are assured of utilizing available resources to greatest advantage.

As decisions are made and council suggestions implemented, periodic reports should be made to the council reporting on any progress that has been made and any problems faced in following through on their recommendations. This gives the council an opportunity to react to stay abreast of the implementation of their suggestion. It also assures a knowledgeable group that understand what cannot be done if there is inadequate funding and insufficient community support.

Once programs are in operation, the group should begin evaluating their effectiveness in terms of the stated initial objectives. As the evaluation continues and the program grows and develops, new problem priorities establish themselves and new program objectives become important. The entire process begins again. With each complete cycle, the community educator can expect greater community input into and involvement in the total Community Education program. This results in Community Education that truly meets the problems and needs of the community — as the members of the community themselves perceive their problems and needs.

SECTION III

Program Development

CHAPTER V

Adult Education

Terms such as Community Education, adult education, and recreation are often used interchangeably and perceived as merely different names for the same thing. Adult educators, for example, look at Community Education and see programs for adults designed to enable them to complete high school, to gain literacy skills, and to develop new interests and talents. Because the programs are identical to ones offered through their own educational system under a program entitled "Adult Education," it is understandable that the conclusion drawn is that they are one and the same.

Recreation directors also observe many recreational programs in schools and see a variety of sports activities being both taught and made available for general participation. Comparing these activities to their own offerings, little difference is observed and the conclusion, again, is understandably the same as that drawn by the adult educator—that there is no real difference between Community Education and school based recreation programs.

There is a very basic difference between Community Education and the programming available through adult education, recreation and the like. This difference is primarily a conceptual one, a difference in goals and objectives, rather than specific differences in existing programs. This difference is observed in the view that one accepts of the entire educational system and the educational role that must be played by it. Similar programs have different purposes and the crucial concern has to be in the differences in purposes that the programs are designed to meet.

Adult education leaders and other program directors develop programs to provide people with activities, skills, new experiences, interests, and a general opportunity to improve and upgrade themselves so that they can live and enjoy life at a higher level. These programs are often highly successful, involve large numbers of people and often do meet the program objectives. Community Education accepts the value of these goals and incorporates these concepts into its general framework. Beyond this, however, another dimension is added. Community educators believe that this initial participation is one means of developing and encouraging deeper involvement of people in improving the community in which they live. The programs that are designed are not an end in themselves, but rather become the entree to a greater individual involvement and contribution to the community.

It is an unfortunate fact that many community educators often do not perceive this differentiation and thus offer a variety of programs that truly are distinguished from adult education or recreation in name only.

It is important to again recognize here that true Community Education is not achieved within a few years. It is a process that must develop slowly and steadily. New Community Education programs often are a number of activities and programs; nothing more. The crucial test, however, is the direction that is being taken. Are the programs being planned to assure deeper involvement later, or are they planned to provide a service to the individual with no further objectives? Participation in classes is not involvement; evidenced daily in colleges and universities. Students attend classes but are not necessarily involved in the life and destiny of the university. Community Education should use classes and activities as a springboard to social action and to get people accustomed to using their schools. The individual growth that results from the class activity is a bonus, not the program objective.

From class activities, adults can become involved in helping plan their educational program, that of their children, and finally become

Adult Education

involved in working toward a better community for both themselves and their neighbors. The dimension Community Education adds is one of concern for the betterment of all people, not just the individual.

Historical Overview of Adult Education

Adult education in America can be traced back to Benjamin Franklin. In 1727, he initiated discussion clubs to explore moral, political, and philosophical problems. C. Hartley Grotten refers to Franklin as the "patron saint of American Adult Education."[1] From this very early beginning, the adult education movement expanded in very diverse and creative directions. This diversity was unified, however, in purpose. The first task of adult education in this nation was the transformation of an entire people from being subjects to being citizens — from perceiving themselves as subservient to an aristocracy, to an acceptance and understanding of freedom and a democratic form of government. [2]

This first attempt at adult education in this nation was obviously successful and assisted the nation in its efforts to become an independent democracy.

By approximately 1810, evening schools were beginning in many of the large public schools. They were unstable in that they were often started, dropped, and started again. While evening schools today are generally accepted as the domain of the adult, the early evening schools were established primarily for working children over twelve years of age. The curriculum was usually a repeat of the day program, stressing reading, writing, and computational skills. As these schools began to stabilize, the age of the student population being served gradually shifted to older teens and young adults. This gradual expansion established the foundation for the present adult education programs in the public schools.

---

[1] Malcolm S. Knowles, *The Adult Education Movement in the United States,* Holt, Rinehart, & Winston, Inc., 1962, p. 11.

[2] Ibid. p. 13.

From this, specific programs were established to meet specific adult needs, such as Americanization classes, vocational training courses, high school completion programs, and special interest courses. The state and federal governments began exhibiting some interest in the education of the adult population, and began making its presence felt. The state governments began by establishing permissive legislation which gave local schools the authority to operate evening schools. This late entry is especially interesting since the governments, in effect, gave permission to do something that had been going on for a number of years. This legislation was followed by mandatory requirements regulating the adult education offerings.

Following this entry into adult education, several states began legislating financial assistance. While most states providing adult education did not establish legislative programs until after 1920, a few earlier notable exceptions do exist. The New York Legislature authorized an expenditure of $6,000 per year in Adult Education and the Rhode Island assembly appropriated $5,000 in 1873 for the same purpose. Once legislation was passed, the fourth stage in the developmental process of state involvement was the establishment of statewide assistance and services through the state departments of education. This fourth stage is extremely important because it incorporates the concept of adult education into the statewide educational structure.

The federal government's first real entry into adult education was in agricultural education. This was initiated with the Hatch Act of 1887, which established agricultural experimental stations within the land grant colleges. This act was followed in 1914 by the Cooperative Extension Act. The Cooperative Extension Act was intended to educate farmers to improve crop yield and farming techniques. Today this effort is heralded as this nation's greatest single adult educational venture, and it's most successful.

More recently, the federal government established the Adult Basic Education Act in an attempt to reduce and ultimately eliminate adult illiteracy. This act and the funding it makes available is presently having a major impact upon the adult education movement in this country.

In reviewing the growth and establishment of adult education in this country, certain basic principles have emerged in public education:

1. Public schools have a responsibility to assist the citizenry in keeping abreast of change within the society. Adult educators have

Adult Education

recognized that the society requires not only a literate population, but an intelligent one that is willing to share responsibility for social progress.

2. Public schools have an important role in training for the wise, purposeful, and enjoyable use of leisure time. The ill-effects of enforced idleness and expanded leisure time can be offset by creative, wholesome recreational activities and educational opportunities.

3. Public schools have a responsibility to provide second chance opportunities to those individuals in the society who, for a variety of reasons, did not complete high school. The problems faced by the nonhigh school graduate are severe and will become increasingly so. Adults must be given the opportunity to obtain the basic high school credentials that are required in the society.

4. The public schools should expand the use of their facilities, personnel, and leadership. They should become more active within, and available to, the community they serve.

5. Because of technological advances and expanding job automation, the public schools should become increasingly involved in vocational training, retraining, and readjustment.

While adult education encompasses a variety of specific programs and activities, this chapter will deal only with those three most often found with the public schools: Adult Basic Education, Adult High School Completion, and Adult Noncredit Special Interest Programs. There are several areas of concern that apply generally to adult education and encompass all three of these areas. The general over-riding discussion areas will be presented first and then specific concerns will be discussed in each of the three adult education areas.

Obtaining the Support of the Board of Education

Once community need has been established and it has been determined that programs should be developed to serve adults in the community, administrative personnel should be included in the planning and development of the program. It is extremely important that the superintendent, high school principal, and other key people be involved at this point, since their support later might be directly linked to their initial involvement. Adequate planning time should be allowed.

After other administrators have been involved in the planning and the data has been presented to them, a decision must be made to either establish a program for adults based on the need demonstrated in the data collected or elect to continue no further if no need is shown. It is important to involve the administrative staff in this decision and reach consensus. Unless administrative personnel believe in the importance and worth of what is being attempted, the program's potential will be greatly reduced. Initial administrative support, on the other hand, will greatly expand the program's chances for success.

Initial Presentation to the Board of Education

If the administration decides to develop programs for adults, an initial presentation should be made to the local board of education. This presentation should not be a detailed description of the proposed program, but rather a summary of the needs demonstrated by the study that was conducted and a general overview of what should be done.

Selection of a person to make the board presentation is crucial. Often the superintendent or the individual assigned to do the initial surveys and groundwork is chosen. A resource person might also be brought in to discuss adult needs in more general terms and to expand the scope of the board's thinking. Some possible choices here are state department of education staff members, adult educators operating successful programs in nearby communities, or a representative of the State Association of Public School Adult Educators.

It is important at this meeting that the board members fully appreciate their responsibility to provide educational opportunities to the entire community. Some general concepts that might be covered at this time include:

A. The need for an opportunity for adults to grow and better prepare themselves for the new challenges of our modern world.

B. The positive effect upon children that will result from having parents interested in education and concerned about it. Statistics

Adult Education

indicate a definite relationship between the educational level achieved by parents and that of their children. It is quite possible, then, that an adult high school completion program will provide a positive influence on the regular day program.

C. The good will that can be developed between the school and adults who have not had positive school experiences and who often have negative feelings toward the school and toward education generally.

D. The advantage of increasing the use of educational facilities.

E. The importance of providing adequate administrative time and resources to allow the program to reach its maximum potential. It is especially important that the time demands upon the individual selected to operate the program be assessed properly for presentation to the board. The amount of time required to administer this program should not be underestimated.

F. A basic understanding of current funds available to operate a program of this nature and anticipated revenues that could be expected once the program becomes operational.

Establishing a Board Policy

After the board of education has accepted the general concept of adult education, work should begin on the establishment of a board policy, which might include:

A. A recognition of the need for educational programs for adults

B. A general statement concerning the purposes to be served by the adult program

C. A brief summary of the general educational philosophy of the board as it relates to this program

D. A listing of the goals and objectives of the program

E. A general statement of support

Student Recruitment

Successful adult education programs do not just happen; they result from careful planning and aggressive recruitment campaigns. It is recommended that assistance from the State Department of Education or neighboring directors of adult education be requested in establishing a recruitment program. This can greatly assist in developing a comprehensive campaign. The following suggestions are made to demonstrate the many recruitment possibilities available. This is not intended to be an all-inclusive list.

Local mass media can be of great assistance. Advertising through brochures, newspapers, matchbook covers, radio, T.V., posters, notices in church bulletins, milk cartons from local dairies and flyers stuffed in grocery bags, can all tell people of the program's existence and provide basic information. In addition, some personal contact can be achieved by recruiting college and high school students for a door-to-door campaign and by asking water and electric meter readers to leave brochures. Neighborhood people may also be used as recruiters. Every recruitment and publicity channel available should be utilized.

Selecting Qualified Teachers

Recruiting a good teaching staff is vital if the program is to succeed. In most instances, the entire program will be evaluated by the adult students as they view the competency of one teacher.

The Michigan Committee on Post-Twelfth Grade Community Education believes that teachers of adults should possess outstanding qualifications in a variety of areas.[3]

"1. *Subject Matter*

The backgrounds of the class entering the adult education program will be broad. Consequently, the mastery of the subject matter on

---

[3] Michigan Department of Education, "The High School Completion Program for Adult and Out of School Youth," Bulletin No. 370 Revised, 1967.

the part of the teacher must be equally broad. Furthermore, in order to meet the challenge which the class will present, the teacher must know his particular field well. Along with the breadth and depth of the subject matter, the teacher must possess an inquisitive mind, a further desire for knowledge, in order to meet the challenge which the class will present."

"2. *Adaptability*

Within each adult education class, there is going to be a wide distribution of ability, interest, and experience on the part of the students. Because of this divergence the teacher must be able to *plan each lesson well so as to meet the needs of all the students.* Besides being a specialist in presenting the particular lesson, the teacher must also be broad enough to encourage different kinds of experiences in the students who lack them. The teacher must be prepared to identify the weak and strong areas of the students and to plan each lesson with these in mind. These will vary with the different classes, and consequently, the teacher must be able to adapt to them."

"3. *Understanding Attitude*

This requirement cannot be overemphasized. Without it a teacher can only meet with failure, while on the other hand, an instructor who possesses this attitude can lead his students a long way with limited capabilities. (A good leader will want to make all his students wish to develop.) The impatience of the student must be met with patience on the part of the instructor. Selfishness and prejudice on the part of the student must be met with tact by the teacher. Of utmost importance is that the teacher learn to compensate in the classroom for his own personal prejudices. He must have an open mind to all students regardless of their ability, interest, age, class, race, or creed. There must be a sincere desire to help each and every one."

"4. *Philosophy*

A teacher must have knowledge of the philosophy or purpose of adult education programs as set forth by the board of education. He should be aware of the needs and problems of the community and be able to present his subject matter in a real and meaningful manner so that he can serve both the student and the community. Unless this cohesive bond is possessed by the teacher, each class becomes an adult education program unto itself and unity of purpose and objectives become lost in a myriad of classes."

"5. *Certification*
It is assumed that all teachers be certified by the proper certifying agency in the state. The requirements for certification of teachers in the adult education program should be broad enough to utilize all those who have demonstrated their expertness or mastery in a particular field. Rather than limiting, the certification code should be so established as to utilize the best resources in the community. In such cases, an emergency certificate should be available to those who have established themselves as capable of presenting a single lecture or series of lectures or demonstrations. Thus, instructors of specific skills might not necessarily hold the same certification as those in the basic curriculum program. Use should be made of specialists or technicians who may not be college educated, but have vocational or special certification by the State Department for their specific assignment."

"6. *Physical Stamina*
Most adult education programs today rely upon teachers other than those regularly engaged in education for their instructors. Consequently, the physical condition of the instructor must be such as to allow him to stand the strain of teaching one or two evenings a week, along with its preparation, after he has already put in a day's work."

"7. *Staffing*
A more desirable situation would be to establish a core of adult education instructors. When programs are not large enough to utilize them full-time it should be possible for them to spend a part of their time teaching in the day program and the remainder in the adult education program. This will make the teacher feel that he is a part of the adult education program and that it is not something done in his spare time."

Teacher In-Service For Adult Teaching

It must be recognized that teaching adult students is quite different from teaching young people. Teachers must respect this difference and act accordingly. Most teachers who are employed in the new adult program have had no experience in teaching adults. Pre-service and in-service training programs are very important in assisting new teachers of adults in dealing with adult needs and problems. Pre-service and in-service techniques are not limited to staff meetings. Staff bulletins, for example, can be an excellent means of communicating different ideas and concepts. "Techniques,"[4] a publication of the National Association of Public Continuing and Adult Educators, specifically deals with the improvement of adult teaching methods and is available for general staff distribution.

The development of a handbook for teachers provides specific information on more routine matters, as well as noting what is expected of the teacher and what can be expected by the teacher. A comprehensive in-service program should be continuous and include teacher visitation and evaluation. This process is discussed in greater detail in Chapter 10.

Facilities and Space

Appropriate facilities and space are extremely important in developing an adult program to meet the needs of adult students. Several considerations should be made:

A. Separate telephone lines should be available to the adult education office and this number should be listed separately in the telephone directory. This gives the adult students a means of direct contact with someone who can give them accurate information. Arrangements should also be made to have the telephone covered during the evening hours when classes are in session.

B. The adult education office should be easily accessible to adults and should be separate from other school offices and classrooms. There should be facilities for private conferences within the office.

---

[4] National Association for Public Adult & Continuing Education, National Education Association, 1201 Sixteenth Street, N.W., Washington, D.C.

C. Adequate seating should be assured, recognizing that adults have difficulty sitting in some of the smaller desks found in schools.

D. Adequate library facilities should be provided. The school library should be open during the times adults are attending classes to the same extent that it is available to youth attending the regular day program. Library holdings should be expanded to meet the needs of the adult students.

E. Since most adult classes are held in the evening, parking lots that are used should be well lighted. Many people will not attend a program if they have to go out into a dark parking lot after class is over.

Developing a Pleasant Atmosphere

As part of developing a pleasant and informal atmosphere, several things should be considered. It is recommended that each school building have a central social area where adults can purchase coffee, rolls, etc. A coffee break should be established during the program to allow a few moments for relaxation and socialization. The central social area should also have smoking facilities. It is important to note, however, that physical facilities alone cannot take the place of the warmth and friendliness of an interested staff.

Establishing Teacher Pay Rates

When establishing pay rates for teachers, it is important to establish hourly rates that are fair and equitable to the teaching staff while commensurate with pay rates normally paid in the area and within the school district. This often presents a problem because of the diversity of pay rates existing in a community between different community agencies and different programs within the school. One agency might pay one rate for a given responsibility and another substantially more or less.

Adult Basic Education

We are rapidly moving to a point in time where the undereducated adult in the United States will have virtually no opportunity to survive in the society on his own. At a time when over 90 percent of the jobs are already available only to the skilled and educated, it takes little imagination to assess the future potential of our illiterate adult five or ten years from now. Adult illiteracy is a very real problem within our society today. The 1960 census indicated that out of an adult population of approximately 99 million, 16.3 million had less than an eighth grade education and according to federal government definitions, were termed functionally illiterate. These figures do not include the substantial numbers of adults completing more than eight grades of formal education, but still functioning below the eighth grade level. It also does not include those adults unwilling to admit to an educational level of less than eight grades. Of this 16.3 million, over 11 million are between the ages of eighteen and fifty-four. They are well within their prime years of productivity.

The Subcommittee on Employment and Manpower stated the problem rather succinctly when they said: "The time appears near at hand when the average worker cannot expect to continue a single occupation for a lifetime. Even if the occupational title does not disappear, the occupational content, over time, is likely to change completely."[5] Senator Vance Hartke then speculates that, "To meet such conditions, adult education is a must. Before the necessary upgrading of technical skills can be effected, there must be an upgrading of basic educational skills for the illiterates. The United States Office of Education now estimates that we have more than 22 million adult functional illiterates in this country, men and women without the equivalent of an eighth grade education."[6]

In an attempt to encourage educational institutions, and specifically public schools, to solve this problem, the United States Congress passed the Adult Basic Education Act. This act provides funds to "encourage and expand basic educational programs for adults to enable them to overcome English language limitations, to improve their basic

---

[5] Vance Hartke, "At the Edge of a Brave New World," *Adult Leadership,* October, 1965, p.118.

[6] Ibid.

education in preparation for occupational training and more profitable employment, and to become more productive and responsible citizens." [7]

Initially, this act was entitled Title II-B of the Economic Opportunity Act and was a part of the much heralded "War on Poverty." In 1966, it became part of the Elementary and Secondary Education Act, administered through the Department of Health, Education, and Welfare; and became "The Adult Education Act of 1966" under this legislation.

Funding for adult basic educational programs is almost completely obtained through this federal enactment. In most states, proposals must be submitted to the State Department of Education describing the local situation faced by the school district, plans for effectively serving that segment of the society that functions at less than an eighth grade level, and a proposed budget that indicates how the district plans to spend money granted to it.

Each state has its own plans and some specific regulations to be met. Anyone planning to initiate adult basic education programs should spend some time learning about the program as it operates in his state and the program priorities established by his State Department of Education.

While each state has criteria unique to its needs and educational philosophy, all plans have some criteria similar to those criteria established by the United States Department of Education in their guidelines. In planning any adult basic education program in which federal funds will be used, the criteria established at the federal level should be considered. Some of these criteria include:

"1. Whether and to what extent a program will serve adults in those geographic areas of the state which have a high concentration of adults in need of basic education.

2. Whether and to what extent a program will serve adults with the greatest basic education deficiencies which are impairing their

---

[7] *A Compendium of Federal Education Laws,* Prepared by Committee on Education and Labor, House of Representatives, May, 1967, p. 335.

ability to obtain employment and become more productive and responsible citizens.

3. Whether and to what extent a program has been planned and/or will be conducted in cooperation with Community Action programs, Work Experience programs, VISTA, Work Study programs, Manpower Development and Training programs, Vocational Education programs, and other programs relating to the antipoverty effort.

4. Whether and to what extent a program will utilize qualified instructional staff, adequate facilities, equipment, materials, and guidance and counseling services.

5. Whether and to what extent a program will provide health information and services to the extent available through cooperative arrangements with state health authorities.

6. Whether and to what extent a program makes provisions for effective recruiting of adults for enrollment.

7. Whether and to what extent a program will provide for use of personnel in college work study programs, VISTA, and other antipoverty programs.

8. Whether and to what extent a program incorporates the results of research, or techniques which have been proven effective.

9. Whether and to what extent a program incorporates innovative or imaginative instructional methods.

10. Whether and to what extent a program provides for effective administration and supervision by the local educational agency to assure efficient and economical operation."[8]

While funding is extremely important to any educational program, it is not the crucial problem faced in adult basic education. The federal

---

[8] *The Federal Register,* Friday, April 21, 1967, Section 166.9, U.S. Government, Federal Register Office, General Services Administration.

Community Education: From Program to Process

government, through State Departments of Education, fund at a level of 90 percent of program cost. The crucial problem in adult basic education is the recruitment and retention of the illiterate adult. This problem increases with the adult's need for literacy training. The adults within the group are generally individuals who have not had positive experience with the school. They did not succeed as youngsters and usually have many misgivings about going back into the same situation in which they previously experienced failure.

While fear is often one important reason why adult illiterates avoid basic education, there is another phenomenon interjected into this avoidance. Phillip Jackson refers to this as the development of a closed-minded system resulting from personal alienation from the society. He feels there are levels of personal alienation toward the world and toward specific things in the world and that as people move through these levels there is an increasingly greater tendency to reject societal values and the values held within societal institutions.[9] This phenomenon is often found among the *undereducated, underemployed,* and unaccepted portion of our society and one of the negative results is the closing of the mind against the value of education and educational and societal goals with those most in need being the most alienated.

While there seems to be no one good way to overcome this problem, there are several recruiting techniques which seem to be somewhat successful. Each incorporates the same basic ingredient — personal contact. The mass media seems to be almost totally ineffective with illiterate adults. Many districts have achieved recruiting success through:

1. *Community Agents*
   Noncertified residents from the community to be served are employed to seek out undereducated adults and encourage them to participate in the programs being offered.

---

[9] William Puder and S. E. Hand, "Personality Factors Which May Interfere With the Learning of Adult Basic Education Students," *Adult Education,* Vol. XVIII, No. 2, Winter, 1968, pp. 88-89.

2. *Teacher Recruiters*
The teacher who will teach the class makes home visits with potential students prior to the first class session. This establishes student-teacher rapport and reduces much of the student anxiety regarding how he or she will be accepted.

3. *Using Students Already in the Program*
A study by the U. S. Office of Education revealed that most students enrolled in Adult Basic Education learned about the program from another student. Once an initial program has been established, the students in the program can become the best possible recruiters.

While many other techniques and combinations of techniques are possible, the preceding examples provide a sufficient base to begin. The important concept to remember is that adult basic education recruitment requires individual contacts combined with patience and persistence.

Once students are recruited for adult basic education, they should begin a program that provides them with much personal satisfaction, a feeling of growth and potential, an ability to better handle problems that are presented daily, and steady observable growth in literacy skills. Obviously, a program of this type takes much planning and consideration. It cannot be done by simply selecting a textbook and a teacher. Like the development of any curriculum, the adult basic education curriculum should be the result of the thinking and study of all teachers involved, the program administrator, and any school service personnel that will either be directly or indirectly involved with the program. It is suggested that prior to the initiation of the project and prior to the submission of a proposal, a planning grant be requested to develop an appropriate curriculum.

Once the program has been established and is in operation, continuous evaluation is crucial. A later chapter will deal specifically with evaluation. It is sufficient to say at this point that the evaluation system must provide continuous and instant feedback to allow program changes whenever it is evident that such changes are warranted.

Adult Basic Education is certainly one of the most difficult areas to program in all of continuing education. One can seldom justify its existence on the basis of extensive program enrollments. In very basic terms, it's the real "guts" of what adult education is all about. It is providing service to those most in need — individuals whose entire lives are dwarfed and diminished by an inadequate education who often do not realize the cause of their dilemma and sometimes actively oppose any attempt to assist them.

Adult High School Completion [10]

Adult high school completion programs have been established to provide second chance opportunities for adults who have not completed high school. This group of adult citizens, along with those adults previously discussed who are in need of basic literacy skills, present many problems to the society in addition to the personal problems they encounter in their daily lives. The Michigan Committee on Post-Twelfth Grade Community Education states the problem that this country faces with undereducated adults very well when they say:

"A. As workers, the undereducated adult is less and less able to meet the rising levels of skill demanded by our improving technology. They are inevitably the last hired, the first fired, and the perennial consumers of our welfare budgets. They lack the basic educational means to take advantage of vocational retraining programs, and become an increasingly larger and harder core of chronically unemployed.

"B. They are less and less able to provide the parental guidance their children need in the face of growing complexities of modern urban life and, under these circumstances, their lack of education diminishes the stability and the beneficial influence of our nation's families, whose vigor undergirds our national virture.

---

[10] Many of the ideas presented in this section of the chapter are the result of the thinking of a committee established by the Michigan Department of Education. This committee was chaired by Dr. Clyde LeTarte. Committee members were: Mr. Don Arsen; Mr. Walter Cooper; Mr. William Dietzel; Mr. Bruce Jacobs; Mr. Kenneth Lane; and Mr. Charles Porter. Appreciation is expressed for the time and effort expended by these committee members.

Adult Education

C. They are less resourceful in using, wisely, the increasing hours of leisure which improved technology and increasing longevity are providing.

D. They are readily exploited by those who prey upon the ignorant and the gullible. They find it difficult to protect themselves, their families, and their communities from irresponsible or malicious propaganda.

E. They provide a weak and shifting element in the foundation of citizen understanding upon which our national leaders depend for support in the complex decisions of the day." [11]

High school completion programs for adults, like any other educational program, must be carefully planned and initiated to attain maximum success. This planning must concern itself with curricular and course content, scheduling, counseling, financing, administration, and promotion. This total program should be planned to assure integration into the total school program. To be successful, it is felt that school districts considering the initiation of a high school completion program for adults should make provisions for one person to be responsible for the program and assure him an adequate amount of time to properly fulfill his responsibilities. At its inception, this individual often is the person responsible for Community Education in the district. As the program matures and expands, it often becomes necessary to employ a director whose total efforts are dedicated to the high school completion aspect of the Community Education program.

The Initial Step: *Determination of Need*

In order to establish an adult high school completion program it is necessary to determine the need within a community for that program. There are two basic questions that must be answered to determine this need: First, how many individuals within a district or area could benefit

---

[11] Michigan Department of Education, "The High School Completion Program for Adults and Out of School Youth," Bulletin No. 370, Revised 1967.

from the proposed service; secondly, how many would be interested in participation should the program be established? There are several available methods of determining need in a community and each method can provide a partial picture of the need as well as information essential to its responsible determination. Some of these methods include:

A. *Census Data*
   Census data are available on a county-by-county basis and provide information on the number of undereducated adults in the county. This information is normally available through the county clerk's office or a local library. Although census data are not always current enough to be completely satisfactory, they do provide some basic information.

B. *School Records*
   1. A review of the school district dropout rate for the past several years provides information concerning the number of potential participants.

   2. Many school registration forms list the highest educational level achieved by both parents.

   3. Most school districts participate in Title I of the Elementary and Secondary Education Act. Much of the data included in Title I proposals include statements related to general educational levels of parents.

C. *Local Resources*
   1. Major employers in a community usually have information concerning the educational levels of their employees. They also have minimal educational levels required for employment, which provide basic information concerning the difference between job requirements and existing levels of education within the community. Interviews with the personnel directors of employers within the area provide valuable insight into the extent of the problems of the undereducated. This contact might also provide a foundation for later joint planning and programming between the school and business and industry.

Adult Education

2. Local social agencies often work with the individuals who may need a high school diploma. Interviews with personnel from the local Employment Security Commission, Welfare and Social Service Agency, and the Community Action Agency can provide information concerning programming needs and additional insight can be gained into the specific needs and concerns of the adults that might be involved.

3. Arranging an interview with the local director of cooperative extension might assist in determining the nature of the community and the possible need for a high school completion program.

4. Many communities have conducted economic studies that provide current information concerning adult educational levels. Visits with local government officials and local chamber of commerce officials will determine if such studies exist and where they might be found.

5. A visit to neighboring districts that offer a high school program to adults might prove beneficial. The local director, for example, might know the number of people from surrounding districts enrolled in his district's program and assist in assessing the need in your district. In making this contact, it might also be possible to establish some type of cooperative effort.

6. Procedures should be established to survey a sample of local adult residents. An attempt should be made to discover how much interest there is in a high school completion program for adults and how many people would participate should a program be offered.

The Second Step: *Planning the Program*

A. *Developing Curriculum and Administrative Policy*

The development of a good initial curricular offering is crucial since much of the success of the program will depend upon it.

1. In determining which classes will be offered initially, an attempt should be made to identify a variety of required courses which all students will need to take such as English, history, and math. A few electives that are likely to be popular should also be included since these classes tend to draw additional adult students into the program. The greater the variety of courses that can be offered initially, the stronger the inducement for additional people to enter the program. The extent of this variety should be tempered by an assessment of the potential first semester enrollment indicated in the need study.

2. Many students will wish to transfer credits earned in correspondence courses into the programs. Others may wish to enroll in correspondence courses through the program to enable them to take special classes that are not being offered. Procedures will have to be developed to handle these situations when they arise. Correspondence courses should be used as a supplement to the regular curriculum — not as a replacement. Regular classes allow the adult student the opportunity for student-teacher-class reaction and interaction and provides an opportunity to expand a rather systemized approach to learning a subject into a more personalized one.

3. In establishing the requirements for graduation, it is important to maintain flexibility and keep the adult problems and concerns in mind. It is also important to note that most existing requirements are designed for a four-year high school program. The trend for adult high school programs, on the other hand, is toward the three-year, twelve Carnegie unit system. This trend assists in maintaining requirements that adult students consider reasonably obtainable.

4. Many different scheduling plans have been established to meet local community needs. Programs vary in time requirements from 45 to 60 hours for each one-half Carnegie unit. Those offering credits with reduced class hours often request additional home study. Within these general plans, some districts provide two to three hours of instruction two nights a week for each course taken while others provide three to four hours of instruction one night a week for each course taken.

5. In planning any high school curriculum, the requirements of regional accrediting associations must be considered. It is important to point out that most accrediting associations recognize that adult high school completion programs should be different from high school programs serving children and recommend that consideration be given to the different needs, problems, and learning patterns of adults.

B. *Granting High School Credit*

Each adult who enrolls in the high school completion program will have had a variety of educational, social and work experiences. Many of these experiences should be considered when granting credit and determining the requirements remaining for graduation.

Granting credits for activities participated in outside the regular high school program allows program flexibility that presents obtainable goals to the enrolling student and reduces the total amount of class time that would normally be required.

In granting credit, the cooperation and understanding of the regular high school principal is essential. He is usually the individual who ultimately accepts or rejects credits. To assist the principal and adult education director in determining credits that shall be granted, it might be helpful to establish an evaluation committee to review individual cases and determine what credit should be granted. This committee could include one or more of the following: the high school principal, the adult education director, the director of vocational education, and a high school counselor serving the adult program. There is also a possibility of granting credit by examination. Test scores from the General Educational Development Test (G.E.D.) are sometimes used as a grade placement device, rather than as a test for high school equivalency. This allows individuals to be placed at higher grade levels than would be normally allowed by simply reviewing completed high school credits.

A specific policy should be established for the acceptance of credits from correspondence schools, business and trade schools, armed service schools, and other public and private agencies offering courses of study. A determination of the number of classroom hours required to receive 1/2 Carnegie unit of credit should be made. It is generally agreed that this should be not less than 45 hours nor more than 60 hours for adult programs.

C. *Student Eligibility*

Questions often arise in adult high school completion programs concerning who is eligible to attend and who is not. This is especially true with individuals under eighteen years of age who have dropped out or have been dismissed from the regular K-12 program. It is important that a policy be developed to handle this situation and that special provisions are made for this age group. Students attending regular day classes often wish to enroll in adult programs for additional credit. Most adult high school programs have provisions allowing this if the high school principal gives his approval. Regular students in parochial or private schools are often encouraged to enroll within their regular school program. Acceptance of these students should also be contingent on the permission of their high school principal.

D. *Establishing an Adult Counseling Program*

1. The establishment of a counseling program as an integral part of the adult high school program is essential. In smaller programs, the adult education director serves as the counselor. In other programs, one or more trained counselors are employed to serve in this capacity. In either case, the contacts that the counselor makes with adults must be enthusiastic, warm, friendly, and encouraging. The first contact is very important, and the adult must feel accepted and encouraged.

2. The initial counseling session should include an explanation of the total program and the general requirements that must be met. Possible methods of reducing the total number of courses required through granting credit for other experiences should be discussed. In the initial counseling session, the counselor should determine what the goals of the enrolling adult are and assess the purpose behind the decision to return to school.

3. It is imperative that a sufficiently large staff of competent counselors be available during the initial enrollment period.

Many interested students might be lost because plans were not made to adequately enroll and counsel students as they enter the program.

4. It is important to establish a record-keeping system to record counseling comments, transcripts, school records, planned programs, and approved credits. Each individual enrolled should have a separate file. Since these records are as important as the cumulative records of any other high school student, it is necessary that they be handled accordingly.

5. Adequate secretarial help must be available to appropriately handle all record-keeping.

6. Within the record-keeping system that is established, provisions must be made for recording and storing a variety of unique and unusual records. Some system of evaluating records and credits should be included, and each student's records should be individually evaluated on the basis of these established criteria.

7. It is also important to have a counseling system established that goes beyond the contact made at initial entry. Once registration is completed and students begin attending classes, counseling contacts must be maintained. Within the first year, an individual program should be established for each student and the evaluation of all credits should be completed.

E. *Selection of Supplies and Materials*

In selecting materials and supplies for the adult program, several considerations should be made. In selecting texts, it is important to give consideration to paperback books and consumable supplies. It is recognized that initially the same texts that are used in the day program might also have to be used for adults. It is important to attempt to move away from this as the desires of the teachers and the needs of the adults become better known. In attempting to determine whether to sell or rent textbooks to adults, provisions should be made to allow any student to buy a book when desired and, where possible, to rent textbooks that students will probably not want to keep. In purchasing these materials from suppliers, one must allow adequate time for delivery.

F. *Financing*

An important part of any program is financing. Many states have committed themselves to varying degrees of support for programs of this type. The Federal Government in its 1970 legislative session established enabling legislation to assist programs designed to provide educational opportunities for individuals with less than a high school diploma. This legislation was an expansion of the Adult Education Act of 1966 and has the very practical effect of establishing a high school diploma as a minimal educational level in this nation. At this point, financial support has not been approved at the federal level even though the recognition of need is now established.

G. *Enrollment Procedures*

It is important to develop enrollment procedures that obtain information important to the program in a brief and concise manner. A pre-enrollment period should be established to assure adequate time to counsel and schedule. It is also quite possible that many people will wait until the first night of classes to enroll. Procedures should be established to allow this to take place and to process these applications quickly.

High School Equivalency Programs

No discussion of high school completion programs would be complete without mentioning the over-increasing trend toward high school equivalency programs. In most states, it is possible to obtain high school equivalency certificates by successfully passing a basic series of tests. The General Educational Development Test, (G.E.D.) is certainly the most common test in use today. Many programs have been established to assist adults in the preparation for this test. These programs vary extensively, from brief cram courses specifically covering only the test material, to programs that are broadly based, providing basic knowledge in a variety of academic areas.

While tests of this nature are recognized as a valuable tool for the community educator in his efforts to assist people to gain the basic credentials necessary in this society, the authors do wish to express some concern. Educators and educational institutions should have goals centering around expanded knowledge, improved ability to cope with the environment, and an increased self-understanding. To establish programs geared to the successful completion of a test, with no real concern for educational goals, seems counter-productive to the purposes of education. High school equivalency programs should be incorporated into the regular educational program and should not be a ten to twenty hour cram session geared for a comparatively meaningless test and certificate.

Adult Noncredit Special Interest Program

The general area of special interest noncredit programs for adults is often the most maligned program area in which adult educators are involved.

Derogatory references to "underwater basket weaving" and other noncredit courses of nonacademic stature are often suggested to the adult educator by other more traditional educators. There seems to be a general feeling among many educators that the "fun" type course offerings or the nonacademic self-enrichment courses are somehow beneath the dignity of the educational establishment and that education, by dirtying its hands in the nonacademic, will somehow be reduced to meaningless trivia. And that the "academic standards" of the institution will become sullied and the educational program will become somehow less valuable.

To state that there is room within the educational system to meet the varied interests of an adult community is certainly not a novel statement. To imply that public schools are justified in providing enriching activities also is not unique. In 1918, the NEA Commission on Reorganization of Secondary Education established seven basic educational principles.[12] These "Seven Cardinal Principles" have been

---

12 Commission on the Reorganization of Secondary Education, "Cardinal Principles of Secondary Education," (Washington, D.C., U.S. Government, Printing Office, 1918).

stressed in university education courses ever since. In fact, they have become an important keystone in our entire educational philosophy. Five of these seven principles include "worthy use of leisure time," "health," "worthy home membership," "citizenship," and "ethical character."

Each of these can be accepted as part of a basic ingredient within a nonacademic activity for adults. Certainly the educational system within this country has not become so stifled and traditional that any hint of enjoyment of learning is perceived as an unworthy use of public education. It is imperative that adult educators recognize the value and worth of special interest courses designed to meet a variety of individual interests, and that they perceive these courses as an important integral part of the total adult educational programs.

Paul Bergevin's statements on the goals of adult education certainly incorporates special interest programming within them:

"A. To help the learner achieve a degree of happiness and meaning in life;

B. To help the learner understand himself, his talents, and limitations, and his relationships with other persons;

C. To help adults recognize and understand the need for life-long learning;

D. To provide conditions and opportunities to help the adult advance in the maturation process spiritually, culturally, physically, politically, and vocationally;

E. To provide, where needed, education for survival, in literacy, vocational skills, and health measures."[13]

To attempt to meet these five major goals exclusively through the academic credit activities would be impossible.

---

[13] Paul Bergevin, "A Philosophy for Adult Education," The Seaburg Press, New York, 1967, pp. 30-31.

Adult Education

While it is virtually impossible to categorize the thousands of noncredit special interest courses and activities that are being taught daily, an attempt will be made to limit this discourse to seven major areas:

1. Programs for the aging

2. Programs in economics and money management

3. Programs providing recreational activities and learning opportunities

4. Programs in public affairs and community development

5. Programs to support and improve the home and family

6. Programs in the arts

7. Programs for providing and expanding vocational competency.

Programs for the Aging

The aging comprise an ever-increasing segment of our society. To ignore their specific educational needs is to ignore the needs of at least eight to ten percent of our total population. Because this group is rather diverse, a variety of programs are usually established to meet some of their specific needs. Carl Minich[14] points out several specific program areas in which adult educators may get involved.

1. Vocational training for supplemental income

2. Cultural activities for expanding and enriching living

3. Health education specifically dealing with health problems faced by the elderly

---

[14] Carl E. Minich, "Major Curriculum Areas and Program Concerns," *Administration of Continuing Education,* Edited by Nathan C. Shaw, National Association for Public School Adult Education, Washington, D.C., 1969, Chapter 9, pp. 194-195.

4. Family life education designed to assist the elderly to adjust to family and social relationships that have changed as a result of aging

5. Community service programs designed to involve the aged person in community betterment and to make him feel a useful part of the society

In planning any program for the aged, the important ingredient is the establishment of close working relationships with a variety of local voluntary and governmental agencies established for the same purpose. Perhaps one of the greatest services adult educators can offer is one of coordination and cooperation. Any program planned through the public schools should be well-integrated into the total program that the community is providing for the aged.

It is also important to involve the aged themselves in the planning. All too often programs have been planned for the group rather than with them and they usually result in dismal failure. People who have not experienced the problems of aging and of retirement simply are not aware of the many unique problems and concerns faced by this group.

One of the greatest services public adult education might provide is in the area of preretirement planning. Existing literature in the field of geriatrics is consistent in stating that the retirements with the fewest problems are those that are planned. Retirements that just happen often result to an extremely unhappy and maladjusted individual.

This program area will become increasingly important to community educators because this age group is a rapidly growing segment of our society. To ignore this very important minority's needs is to ignore a large population segment that has many needs and concerns that might be answered through the public educational system.

Programs in Economics and Money Management

Programs in this area are extremely diverse, providing opportunities in basic home money management at one end of the continuum to discussion series on major economic issues at the other. Each, however, has one basic ingredient — better coping with the economic structure in the American society. Since varying economic needs require diverse

Adult Education

programming, the many people that are attracted to the programs are also quite diverse. In planning specific programs within this general heading, it is important to identify the client to be served and specifically determine his unique needs. Once this has been established, specific programs will follow.

It is also important to enlist the variety of community agencies already involved. Involvement in program planning avoids costly duplication, overlapping, and program voids. Some of the community agencies that probably provide educational offerings of some type within the general framework of economic education include: Labor Unions, YMCA, YWCA, Chamber of Commerce, Cooperative Extension Agencies, Community Action Against Poverty, Community College Adult Education Programs, University Extension Programs, and various Social Welfare agencies.

Programs Providing Recreational Activities and Learning Opportunities

Individuals within our society are increasingly obtaining more and more leisure time opportunities. As a result, literally millions of people are attempting new activities, learning new sports, and developing a variety of skills and talents. The public school, with its extensive physical plant and variety of resources provides a natural center for this development. Programs, then, should be developed to maximize participation opportunities for individuals and community groups interested in using this leisure time in pursuit of recreational goals. Like many other areas of adult education, a variety of agencies are already involved. Many of these agencies utilize school facilities as part of their program.

Recreational programs generally fall into two general categories, participatory and skill development. Participatory programs allow the individual to participate in a skill in which he or she is already somewhat proficient. Skill development programs provide instructional opportunities for individuals desiring to learn specific skills. The main purpose of these classes is preparatory rather than providing the opportunity to participate in a given activity.

This distinction of ten provides a rather natural division of labor between educational institutions involved in recreational programming and their community agencies involved in similar offerings. Educational institutions, by their very nature seem to naturally categorize themselves into the skill development area and other community agencies into the programming of participatory activities. Therefore, while the school might offer a course teaching the techniques of golf, of how to play bridge, or how to knit, or in the fundamentals of public speaking; the Recreation Department of the city or county might establish a golf league; the YWCA a bridge tournament and knitting and social get-togethers; and local drama clubs, opportunities to participate in plays and community theatre presentations.

Because of the variety of programs that can be offered under the general heading of Recreation Programs, it is necessary that each participating agency's role be clearly defined. This important programming aspect of Community Education and the need for a clear role determination is discussed in more depth in Chapter 6.

Programs in Public Affairs and Community Development

We have indicated in the first few chapters the complexity of the present society and the problems that are present as a result. Because we exist within a democracy, it is crucial that the public schools play an active role in encouraging public involvement in local, state, and national problems. The many diverse problems which are found in our society tend to encourage individual and group avoidance of societal problems while requiring greater and greater individual and group concern and involvement. Any public affairs program that is established must have, as one of its major goals, the greater involvement of citizens is finding their own solutions to public problems. Programs of this type, if they are to be meaningful, often cannot be lumped with other course offerings and be presented on a specific time schedule. The very nature of the problem-solving approach eliminates the structured formal classroom-type situation. Public affairs and community development programs established within a Community Education program should be the result of citizen involvement in problems about which they are concerned. The program should be informal, flexible, and changing, meeting the needs and concerns of the participants.

Most public affairs programs are somewhat formalized discussion groups, or a variation of a lecture-discussion series. While these serve a definite purpose, groups dedicated to a problem-solving approach are the vital vibrant forces within the program.

Adult Education

Lest there be a misunderstanding, it should be stated that what is proposed is not easy. Involvement is extremely difficult to achieve. Program direction is vague and frustrating because people are not used to nondirectional situations. The problems that are discussed are often social issues that schools have historically avoided. There are enough problems involved to discourage anyone from starting. But, the reward for meeting these problems is the establishment of the basis for a dynamic, stimulating and meaningful Community Education program.

Programs to Support and Improve the Home and Family

One of the results of our rapidly changing technological society is the disintegration of the family unit. Families are increasingly separated because of varying interests and societal requirements unique to each family member. Programs designed to strengthen this unit provide a great service not only to the family involved, but to the health of the total community as well. Generally, programs established to improve the family are of two types: activities designed for family participation, and classes designed to assist parents or children to improve their relationship within the family and their understanding of their role within it.

Programs for Art Appreciation and Participation

One of the criticisms often leveled at the American citizen is that he lacks an appreciation and understanding of the arts. While many feel the criticism is unjust, the important point is that there is an important role for the school to play in the development and encouragement of the arts and art appreciation. This category normally includes music, painting, sculpture, and other "accepted art forms." Programming in these areas is certainly important, but many other less sophisticated and equally expressive art forms should also be encouraged. Programs in arts and crafts, lapidary, photography, home decorating, and interior design provide an expressive outlet and have popular appeal. Programs designed for the general public in the arts should not be limited exclusively to the "culturally acceptable," but rather broadened to include any activity that allows one to express natural artistic feelings.

It is also important to differentiate between programs designed to be participatory and those designed to develop appreciation. Many individuals are interested in developing and expanding artistic talents. Many others, however, are interested in enjoying other people's talents and expanding their appreciation of these talents.

Programs for Providing and Expanding Vocational Competency

One of the results of technological progress within the society is the rapid obsolescence of occupations. Jobs that existed ten years ago have been automated out of existence. Jobs that will be available ten years from now have not been dreamed of yet. While it is interesting to speculate on whether this is progress or not, or whether it is good or bad; the facts, in very simple terms, indicate that unless workers are continually retrained they will become as outdated as the machines they are now operating.

That public education has a major responsibility in assisting in this retaining is seldom debated anymore. The extent of that involvement and the extent of the responsibility the schools should accept is still very much in question.

Because of the importance of this general area (determining whether or not a person will be employable), no standard formula can be established for initiating these programs into a Community Education program.

Some general guidelines, however, should assist in planning an approach.

Initially, a careful study should be made of the community including a determination of unemployment rates, existing business and industrial needs, existing programs presently operating, reasons for employment, and the perceptions of those working daily with the problem as to what should be done. This could be done under the auspices of a community council, if one exists. Once this information is collected, a coordinating body should be established representing the many organizations and community businesses directly involved in occupational training. This group should review the study, establish program priorities, and attempt to determine how the retraining needs of the community can best be met.

The school's role in this retraining process will vary from community to community, depending upon the vocational needs of the community, the availability of adequate vocational facilities and equipment, and the extent of involvement of other organizations in the retraining process. School officials can provide a major service function to communities merely through coordination. In most instances, schools will also provide some of the vocational programming. Unless extensive vocational facilities are available, the public school input into the training process normally is quite basic.

By combining all vocational efforts in a community and looking for areas of overlap and overlook, expanded opportunities are developed through shared programming and shared use of existing facilities.

While the extent of the actual programming role varies from community to community, if vocational coordination does not exist in a community, there is no question that the community educator should accept the responsibility of attempting to change this. Community Education leaders should accept the responsibility initiating the needs study, encouraging and stimulating interest, and developing and maintaining cooperative programming.

Summary

Adult noncredit special interest programs are as diversified as the interests of the community. Each specific program offering is legitimate in its own right if there is an interest in the community for it. While the public schools have a variety of natural opportunities and reasons for establishing programs of this type, it is crucial that they avoid duplication of and competition with programs offered through existing community agencies. In most communities, there are always more activities that should be offered than money to provide them. By avoiding duplication, the joint offering of many community agencies can be far more extensive than programs available through competing agencies trying to establish their own pre-eminence in given area.

CHAPTER VI

Recreation

Recreational programming within Community Education, like any other well-planned program opportunity, requires much thought and planning. The establishment of objectives and an understanding of why recreational opportunities are important to the health of a community is even more important than in most other program areas that we have discussed. This is true because using tax money for "fun and relaxation" seems somehow frivolous to many people – especially to the people who do not participate in recreational activities.

It is the purpose of this chapter to establish a basic philosophy of recreation and then present some general guidelines for the establishment of recreational programs. The concepts and guidelines presented will not be all-encompassing because of the unique and individual recreational requirements and existing opportunities within any given community.

Establishing a Philosophy of Recreation

While writers in the field of recreation tend to disagree on which agency or agencies should provide the bulk of recreational opportunities in a community, they do seem to agree upon the reasons for providing recreational opportunities:

A. Our society is increasingly becoming a sendentary one. This is most evident in the spectacular rise of spectator sports over participatory activities. For very basic health reasons, the human body requires physical activity. Man is a total unit and to operate at peak performance, all parts of the being must function properly. To reduce the effectiveness of any one part of that unit reduces the effectiveness of all other parts. As man's physical capacity deteriorates, it directly and indirectly affects his emotional and intellectual capacities. A variety of recreational opportunities provides an opportunity for physical fitness and offers encouragement for a more active use of leisure time.

B. As the society becomes increasingly complex, individual tensions and strain increase. Man must have a release from the variety of pressures that modern society places upon him. Recreational opportunities can provide this release either through physical exertion or through the expansion of interests that make it possible to get away from everyday troubles and concerns.

C. Much has been written about the depersonalization of the society. As our society has grown larger and more complex and we are forced to live in closer and closer proximity to our fellow man, we have tended to emotionally and intellectually build more barriers between ourselves and those living and working around us. Recreation provides a positive opportunity to reverse this trend and improve a community's chances to have positive personal interaction. Socialization opportunities can be provided through recreation, and as a result, individuals get to know their neighbors.

D. From the beginning of the human race, man has sought to achieve new skills, new thoughts, and new and better ways of living. He has always been interested in growth. While some may call this instinct natural competitiveness and, others, man's personal desire to grow as an individual, the fact remains that human beings do have a normal desire to achieve that which is beyond their present level of proficiency. A good recreation program provides an opportunity to both learn new skills and to improve existing skills through practice.

E. Technology has brought a mixture of blessings and problems. One of the negative aspects of technology is the suppression of individual identity. Human beings become an integral part of a larger, complicated process and often feel stifled and anonymous as a result. Recreation provides the opportunity each human needs to excel in something—develop some unique skill or talent that sets him apart from other people. This uniqueness, this positive individualism, provides a counter balance against the depersonalization of the society and gives individuals a better opportunity to perceive themselves positively.

Defining Recreation

Within these five basic reasons for providing recreational opportunities rests the basic philosophy of a good recreational program. Most writers in the field seem to generally concur about the nature of recreation.

". . . . . recreation is looked upon as activity voluntarily engaged in during leisure and motivated by the personal satisfactions which result from it. Recreation can be physical, mental, social, or a combination of all three. It can be organized or unorganized, planned or spontaneous, undertaken by individuals or groups, and stimulated, sponsored or provided by public, private, voluntary, or commercial interests. In any event, it is always a form of human expression and an influence on personality development." [1]

"Recreation is defined as a field of activities, freely chosen, possessing potentialities for the enrichment of life through the satisfaction of certain basic individual needs and the development of democratic human relations." [2]

". . . . any activity pursued during leisure, either individual or collective, that is free and pleasureful, having its own immediate appeal,

---

[1] *The Recreation Program,* The Athletic Institute, Chicago Illinois, 1954, p. 1.

[2] Howard S. Danford, *Recreation in the American Community,* Harper and Brothers, New York, 1953, p. 120.

not impelled by a delayed reward beyond itself or by any immediate necessity. Recreation includes play, games, sports, athletics, relaxation, positiveness, certain amusements, art forms, hobbies, and avocations. A recreational activity may be engaged in during any age period of the individual, the particular action being determined by the time element, the condition and attitude of the person, and the environmental situation." [3]

There seem to be five general characteristics shared in each definition. They are:

A. Recreation is a freely chosen, voluntary activity. People participate because they want to.

B. Recreation provides personal satisfaction to participants and immediate gratification for their efforts. People feel good while they are participating and afterwards.

C. Recreation is comprehensive in that it includes a variety of activities—physical, mental, or social.

D. Recreation provides opportunities for personal growth and development.

E. Recreation is all-inclusive. No age group is specified as a primary target group and no age group is excluded.

The scope of recreation as defined by people dedicated to the field of recreation indeed seems extensive. Far more extensive, in fact, than the role usually ascribed to it by community educators. This difference in role perception is a crucial one for the community educator to understand as he works with various community recreation leaders interested in serving the recreational needs of the community. The recreation leader's perception of what recreation is is often broad and encompassing, because he perceives recreation in the broadest sense. The community educator's idea of what recreation is tends to be

---

[3] Martin H. and Esther Neumeyer, *Leisure and Recreation,* The Ronald Press, New York, 1958, p. 17, ... a quote from (by permission of) Dictionary of Sociology, edited by Henry Pratt Fairchild, pp. 25-52, copyright, 1944, Philosophical Library, New York.

Recreation

narrower because the diversity and scope of his other general areas of programming tend to overlap into recreation. Because he is responsible for many activities other than recreation, he tends to narrowly define the limits of each program. Because many community educators have a general area of responsibility entitled, "Recreation," along with several other categories of responsibility, they tend to narrow their concept of what recreation is to fit their general program descriptions. While there is nothing basically wrong with this, very real problems can develop if this limited perception of recreation is held as the school begins working with other agencies in establishing good community recreation. As a director with a limited perspective of recreation begins working and discussing shared recreational programming with agencies that have a much broader concept of what recreation is will be a discrepancy in the perceptions of what programs and responsibilities should be shared. The recreationist will perceive a responsibility for activities in many areas which the community educator might designate as adult education or student enrichment. Perhaps an example would help at this point.

One community educator in establishing a Community Education program in a city where an extensive recreation program previously existed, met with the recreation director to discuss mutual interests and possible joint planning. As a community school director, the author had established the concept of recreational programs as those programs involving participatory physical activity and had excluded physical activity resulting from learning situations. For example a golf match was considered recreation, but a class in golf designed to teach basic rules and to improve skills was considered adult education. The recreation directors' perception of recreation incorporated both activities under recreation. When discussion began, the terms *recreation, mutual planning,* and *comprehensiveness* had entirely different meanings. Because of these initial conceptual differences, as discussions continued, mistrust developed. The recreation man began feeling that he was being ascribed a rather miniscule role and the community educator began feeling that the recreation man was empire-building and attempting to establish himself in the field of adult education. It was fortunate for the community that the two men had known each other previously and could state their concerns frankly, or it is very possible that two agencies that should naturally operate in close harmony would have been separated by misunderstanding and a lack of trust.

The important point is not that one definition is inherently better than another, for they both served the purposes of the individuals involved, but that community educators must understand that there is a broader more encompassing veiw of recreation than their own and that they must be willing to accept and respect this as they begin planning the best recreational program possible for the entire community. The best recreation programs are those incorporating as many agencies as possible. Great diversity and choice in recreational offerings is best achieved through diversity in the groups and agencies providing the services, each coordinating its efforts with the others. The community educator should perceive his role as an initiator and coordinator, as well as a recreation provider. The more programs provided by other agencies, the more extensive the resources the community educator has for other areas of need.

Meyer and Brightbill discuss five basic principles in establishing recreational programs in a community:

1. That anything and everything that is done should have its base in the community;

2. That there should be ample recreational opportunities for all the people – children, youth, and adults in all economic and social strata;

3. That the talents of people and the natural resources of the community should be used to the fullest extent;

4. That the program should function through all types of agencies, public, private, and commerical;

5. That recreation should be recognized as an essential force in the life of the people for what it contributes to social well-being." [4]

The remainder of this chapter will attempt to provide some insights as to how these five principles can be incorporated into the

---

[4] Harold D. Meyer and Charles K. Brightbill, *Community Recreation, A Guide to Its Organization,* Prentice-Hall, Englewood Cliffs, New Jersey, 1956, p. 46.

Recreation

establishment of an effective community recreation program. As is the case with any well-developed program area in Community Education, joint planning and community involvement are essential. While the specifics of involvement may vary from community to community, we would like to suggest a general plan to be initiated by community educators in any given community. This suggested generalized approach does provide latitude for the unique differences found in different communities.

Since cooperative action is the key to a good community recreation program, the community educator has a very natural beginning point—finding out how much cooperation does exist between agencies and organizations providing recreation to the community. This can be done rather comprehensively by:

1. Listing all public, private, and volunteer organizations providing any type of recreation

2. Determining the extent of involvement of each by finding out how much is spent per year and the number of people to be served (a private golf club in the community might expend substantial sums of money, but limit its services to a rather exclusive group)

3. Listing specific programs provided through each group and then determining their general areas of recreational service

4. Doing some comparative analysis of the various programs provided and finding specific areas of overlap. This should be coupled with an attempt to determine those areas that are being overlooked—resulting in a void in the total recreational program. There are often many people left out of a comprehensive program because they have unique recreational needs. Senior citizens, for example, cannot compete with younger people and therefore need special activities geared to their abilities.

Once the study has been completed and the information completed it should be shared with those agencies primarily responsible for the community's recreation and any existing recreational councils or committees. The community educator will be forced to select some agencies and exclude others, simply because of the large numbers involved. The group of people that should be invited to a meeting to discuss recreational findings should be those most interested and most involved. Labor unions provide recreation, for example, but not as a primary purpose of the organization. In limiting the size of a recreational group, organizations involved on a secondary basis should be excluded before groups such as the YWCA, for example, that have recreational opportunities as a primary goal.

The recreation group finally invited should be somewhere between 5 and 20 in number, depending upon the size of the community and the extent of existing recreational programs.

The first meeting should consist of a presentation of the data that has been collected and a statement of concern by the community educator that recreational services in the community could be expanded and money more wisely spent through cooperative efforts. At this point, the meeting should be opened to discuss concerns, ideas for the future, etc. It is important to note that no suggestion has been made for the community educator to present a possible plan of action or some "recommendations" with his presentation. This should be avoided. It is important to keep in mind the nature of the group. Each organization has operated independently in the past, providing one or more services to the community. Each has worked to establish the programs that they are providing. The mere presentation of the data that has been collected and the suggestion of possible change is enough to trigger many defense mechanisms within the group. Any further statement by the community educator regarding what should be done might be perceived as an attempt by the school to "take over." The community educator might very well lose the group at this point, should he try to present his "solution" to the problem.

It is suggested instead that the director merely act as a moderator in the beginning, encouraging a variety of ideas and concerns and attempting to summarize these for the group. As these ideas develop and take shape, the community educator, as moderator, should work toward a next step—where do we go from here? Upon achieving this, the meeting can end upon a successful note with all concerned feeling that something was accomplished and that there is more to come.

Once the initial meeting is over and the group begins to assume an identity of its own, the community educator should attempt to ease out of the leadership position he has established and establish a participatory position equal to each of the other participants. When this has been achieved, he can begin injecting his personal concerns, his ideas, and his thinking concerning the direction the group should be taking.

One last word of caution should be emphasized at this point. During the period of time when data is being collected, it is extremely easy for the community educator to draw conclusions and to begin to establish a general plan for the community in his mind. As a result of this, it is quite possible that he will have established a direction that he hopes the recreation group will take when he attempts to bring them together. This must be guarded against. The moment a group perceives that the community educator is attempting to gain acceptance for some previously established plan and to use them as a group merely to rubber stamp his plan, his effectiveness is ended. Instead, it is suggested that he enter these meetings with a willingness to accept what develops naturally, convinced that group decision-making process does result in an eventual decision that is best for the community.

Once a recreation council has been established, the community educator should next attempt to establish a Citizen's Recreation Advisory Group. This group should be representative of the community and serve as a sounding board for the council. It may be incorporated into an existing community council, be developed as a subcommittee of the council, or operate as a separate body. Obviously, there are advantages in tying all efforts to a larger coordinating body. The advisory group, whatever the make-up, can assist in evaluating the effectiveness of recreation in the community, in planning programs, in identifying new areas of concern, and in relating to the community what the recreation council is attempting to do. Care should be taken to spell out the specific purposes of the advisory group and the extent of its responsibility. Equal care should be taken to avoid any possibility of the group becoming a rubber stamp for the recreation council. Just as diversity and discussion are good for the council, diversity and discussion within the advisory group are also important.

Once these groups have been established, on the basis of representation, trust and respect, the recreation opportunities presented to the community will flourish. From this base, specific program decisions, such as, who should offer what program or who should pay for what, can be resolved. This is no attempt to present utopia or suggest that upon following these suggestions an ideal program will develop.

Community Education: From Program to Process

It is suggested, however, that if the various recreational agencies within a community can develop programs based on cooperation, the negative aspects of such a venture will be far outweighed by the positive benefits to the community.

CHAPTER VII

Student Enrichment

The third general program area normally considered an integral part of Community Education is student enrichment. This term normally encompasses a variety of special activities available to school age youth preceding or following the regular school day, on weekends and during the summer. While most community educators accept this program phase as a legitimate part of Community Education, few ever attempt to establish reasons for its existence or goals and objectives to be accomplished. Student enrichment has tended to be that programming phase that is done primarily because everyone else seems to be doing it, rather than because of its legitimate value and pre-defined purposes.

To initiate any discussion on student enrichment it is necessary to begin with the students themselves; to look at their needs, concerns, desires, and problems, and to attempt to then review the existing curriculum and analyze how well these needs, concerns, desires and problems are being met by the educational institution.

Earl Kelly in his book entitled, *In Defense of Youth,* believes that, more than anyone else, youth needs a bona fide place in our society. He further states that as a result of the expansion of technology and resulting expanded requirements for participation in the society, that

Community Education: From Program to Process

the only place that this bona fide place can be provided—be assured—is in the public schools, that somehow the public schools must provide youth an opportunity to feel that the school is his—to meet his needs and to serve him. [1]

While one may or may not agree with Mr. Kelly's basic assumption, it is difficult to disagree that there must be something underlying our present youth alienation which has resulted in developing a youth drug culture, a rejection of social norms, and the establishment of a youthful culture possessing an embryonic revolutionary character. If nothing else, Mr. Kelly's observations do lead one to consider today's youth in light of the school's responsibility to them, and to attempt to look at existing curriculum and assess it in light of youthful meaningfulness and relevance. While one may argue whether the school should or should not be youth's new reason for being, it is difficult to debate the need for expanded relevancy and the development of new concerns for meeting educational needs.

In reviewing our existing curriculum it rapidly becomes evident that, at the very least, educational change and innovation have not kept pace with social change, and that certainly some degree of irrelevancy exists between what is taught and what needs to be taught to successfully cope with living in our modern society. The traditional curriculum has been patched, twisted, added to and subtracted from, but has not basically changed. This has resulted in an attempt to present increasing amounts of knowledge in a time span that has remained constant and sometimes shortened; in subject areas that often are outdated and of little real concern to the student.

The consequence of this is the establishment and entrenchment of an intellectual rather than an educational institution with a resulting imbalance favoring the academic aspect of learning at the expense of the social, cultural, and vocational.

It is not the purpose of this chapter to present a critical review of American education, but instead to recognize some serious short-

---

[1] Earl Kelly, *In Defense of Youth,* Prentice-Hall, Inc., Englewood Cliffs, New Jersey, 1962, pp. 30-37.

Student Enrichment

comings, attempt to discuss them, and offer some suggestions for improvement. American education has often stressed the importance of developing the social and moral character of students as well as the academic. This need exists today more than ever before, especially with the increasing complexity of our society and the increasing need for citizens to know how to relate to each other. It seems important, then, that community educators attempt to answer several questions when planning student enrichment activities:

1. What can be done in planning student enrichment programs to broaden the existing curriculum—to expand the limited concept of a six hour educational day and a nine and a half month educational year?

2. What can be done through special programming to attempt to balance the academic side of education with a more socially oriented approach—to provide opportunities for cultural enrichment, recreational interests, and expanded educational enrichment?

3. How can students and community be incorporated into program planning to assure the establishment of a program relevant to their needs and concern?

These questions can best be asked in relationship to the existing curriculum provided in a given school district, the nature of the local community being served by the school, and the nature and needs of the student group to be served.

Planning a Student Enrichment Program

Based upon the preceding statements, there are several reasons for providing students with an extended voluntary program. These include:

1. Providing an opportunity for youth to expand and improve their social skills. These skills include the ability to cooperate in following group rules, to learn the give and take of everyday living, and to learn to better relate to other human beings. These skills are often ignored in the traditional classroom setting where greater stress is placed on more academic concerns.

2. Provide students with an opportunity to pursue their own goals and to expand their abilities in areas of their own choice, as dictated by their personal interests. This includes providing an opportunity to try out new courses and new techniques; and to have the opportunity to fail without feeling like a failure.

3. Provide an opportunity for extensive recreational activity. The need to release excess energy is felt by youth more than any other group and certainly recreational equipment and facilities owned by the public school should be used as extensively as possible for this purpose.

4. Providing a school that assures a positive force in the students' lives. Extended programs assist in improving attitudes toward school and developing positive feelings toward education.

5. Provide an informal friendly educational atmosphere, free of academic structure, where teachers and students can get to know each other on a personal one-to-one basis. The establishment of this relationship should carry over into the regular academic program.

Assuming that any student enrichment program should respond to these basic ingredients, it becomes crucial to assure their consideration from the planning stage through the operational stage.

It has been previously suggested that student enrichment should broaden and expand existing curriculum. By tying the student enrichment program to the existing curriculum, the scope of the educational offering can be broadened while maintaining an orderly learning process. To do this, the community educator must spend many long hours with the director of curriculum, establishing basic educational principles and guidelines to be followed. This should not be done to limit the community educator in program development, but rather to assure consistency and continuity throughout the entire educational process. Once the basic curricular principles have been established, it becomes necessary to determine what students want and need from the program in rather general terms, and, specifically, what activities and programs they desire. This should be done at each local school to assure meeting the unique programming needs of the students in each individual school. No one technique works best for this, and a variety of methods have been used: surveys, use of existing student councils, establishment of new student advisory committees, or just talking informally with a number of students.

After principles have been established as basic guidelines for programming, and interests and needs of students have been determined by students themselves, the task then becomes one of getting the professional staff of the school to develop programs around student interests and needs within these basic curricular guidelines. This planning can often best be done through a small committee of teachers and administrators from the building, who have expressed a specific interest either in curricular improvement or in the Community Education program. Once this group has established a student enrichment program, they can then assist in assuring the total acceptance of the program by the remainder of the teaching staff by providing a base of support within the instructional staff. Once the basic program has been established and staffed, some means should be developed to assure continuous student and teacher feedback. The single question that always must be asked and answered is: to what extent is the program reaching the goals it was established to reach? Again, this can be done informally through discussion and subjective evaluation, or quite formally through rather sophisticated evaluative techniques. The significance of evaluation, whether simple or sophisticated, is improvement in the program.

General Activity Categories

There are five general categories for most student enrichment programs. Each of the five provide very specific benefits to the participants and expand the educational program in rather diverse and unique ways.

1. Many, if not most, of the student enrichment programs provided through public schools are based solely on one premise: they must be fun. Within this fun category, a host of recreational programs are possible. Some of these include: badminton, teen dances, table games, ping pong, basketball, football, arts and crafts, swimming, and roller skating. There are literally thousands more.

   While students participate in these activities only because they enjoy them, many subtle but very real educational benefits accrue.

One of the most important of these is the establishment of a more positive feeling toward the school. The more a child enjoys himself within the school, the more positive the feelings he develops for the entire educational program. Human beings establish positive or negative feelings toward something by weighing the good against the bad and then generalizing either a positive or negative feeling about the whole. The more positive experiences that educators can provide within the educational framework, the better the chance of assuring a generalized "good" feeling about the total educational process.

2. A variety of student enrichment programs are designed primarily as skill development programs. While these activities are also perceived as fun by the students, they do provide an additional dimension. They allow the student a chance to learn or improve a skill, and add breadth to his or her scope of interest. Many of the skills learned in this type of activity can be carried over into adult life. Some courses providing these skills might include sewing, cooking, woodworking, model building, knitting, etc.

3. Many student enrichment activities are designed around existing curricular offerings in the regular day program. These activities attempt to provide an additional dimension to a specific subject area through approaches quite different from those used in the regular program. Math for fun, for example, might be developed around math games and puzzles, and an elementary science for fun activity might be centered around laboratory experimentation which the day program is unable to provide. Often this type of student enrichment activity expands and encourages student interest in specific subject matter areas. It also provides an opportunity for students who were forced to choose one subject over another during the regular school day to now obtain both.

4. A student enrichment activity that has not been developed as completely as some, but certainly possesses an exciting potential are student service oriented programs. These programs attempt to add the dimension of service to others. While a variety of successful programs do exist, a good example of what can be done

by getting students interested in assisting others was demonstrated by a teen service club called the Pacemakers. Some of the activities sponsored by this group include:

A. Sponsorship of three disadvantaged children to a camp

B. Providing a summer field trip for 60 youths

C. Providing free babysitting services and a car pool to aid people in voting

D. Providing and showing educational movies on crime and narcotics

E. Replacing or paying for new nets on all outdoor basketball courts

F. Making a down-payment on a halfway house for ex-convicts and assuming the mortgage. Once the house was purchased, club members contributed time and effort to reconditioning the house themselves. [2]

5. The fifth general category of student enrichment are those programs established to assist students with special problems. These programs, while usually focusing on learning difficulties, might also be developed to assist in the physical or emotional development of children with special problems. An example of this was the establishment of a special program in one community in the form of a tutorial program for disadvantaged youth with average intelligence, but very low achievement scores and grades. This program established a tutorial process in the homes of the children. Tutorial groups were established, when possible, among existing friendship groups and these groups were hosted by parents. They met three times a week for a study session with a teacher. After, parents provided refreshments. This approach not

---

[2] Leslie Ollie, "Study of Selected Aspects of the Community Education Program in Benton Harbor, Michigan," State Human Resources Council, Lansing, Michigan. Unpublished.

only assisted the children academically and socially but also assisted the parents in learning what was required to assure success for their child and provided them an opportunity to participate in their child's learning. A final reward at the end of the year for the tutorial groups was a trip to a professional baseball game for the boys and a visit to a major museum for the girls.

It is important to note that this program was designed for a very specific purpose—to assist under-achieving children with average intelligence in improving their achievement level. Many programs can be designed to meet the unique specific problems of other school age youngsters.

Programming for student enrichment is an extremely difficult and important process, yet one that is often ignored, or at best, given only cursory attention. This is unfortunate because student enrichment can tie the Community Education program of the public schools to the existing curriculum and achieve a first step toward positive curricular change better than any other program segment provided through Community Education.

CHAPTER VIII

Public Relations and Community Education

Public relations has become an integral part of American education. While many taxpayers decry the expenditure of public monies for public relations purposes, its growth and scope in education is evidenced by the existence of a National School Public Relations Association. Public relations, for good or ill, is an integral part of public education and always has been. Any agency, business, or organization has a public relations image, even when they do nothing actively to promote. The public, through a variety of information sources, establishes mind sets about organized structures. Business and industry attempt to present positive information about themselves in an effort to counteract any negative public perception of them that might exist—perceptions that may or may not be true. The public school, though it is an institution established to benefit the public, has similar problems. The citizenry does establish mind sets about education generally and about specific schools or school systems in particular. These feelings are often based upon inaccurate information, rumors, and distortions of truth designed to support a particular pressure group's position. By totally ignoring public relations as a legitimate school function, educators simply leave the public to draw whatever conclusions they wish, based upon any information that happens to be available. Instead of establishing a base of correct information and a positive presentation of the educator's position, this approach leaves the development of public opinion to chance.

A good school public relations program is of great importance to a school district. Not only does it assist in eliminating negative unsupported feelings about the school, it can also assist in creating positive support for educational change, curriculum improvement, and community involvement. In short, a good school public relations program should assist in creating a climate within the community that supports and encourages good education. It should assist in changing public support from that of "grudgingly supportive" to "approvingly supportive," resulting from a clear public understanding of what is going on and what is being attempted.

Many school districts feel that a good public relations program centers around the need for public schools to put their best foot forward, to brighten their image, or to somehow "sell" the public. Any program attempting to do only this will never totally succeed, will never have the impact upon education that it should, and at best, will only put a little glitter and tinsel around the existing school program. A good public relations program cannot just sell. Good public relations requires a two-way communication. Learning what the community wants, needs, and hopes for, and incorporating this into the educational system is as much a part of public relations as telling what the schools are doing.

Two-way communication is the basis for all good public relations. This is spelled out rather succinctly by Merle Sumption and Yvonne Engstrom in their book on school and community relations when they state:

> "The typical school-community relations approach has been predicated on the necessity of bringing the community along with predetermined school plans and program. The approach has been one of 'selling' rather than 'buying' of telling rather than asking." [1]

---

[1] Merle R. Sumption and Yvonne Engstrom, *School-Community Relations – A New Approach,* New York: McGraw Hill Book Co., 1966, p. 147.

They go on to state that there are four essential principles underlying good community school relations: [2]

1. The public school is a public enterprise. It belongs to all members of the public and is their means of achieving social goals important to them. Because the public owns the public schools, it has a responsibility toward the schools that requires them to be knowledgeable and involved in its operation.

2. Public schools are responsible for the maintenance of academic freedom; for providing an atmosphere of free inquiry and a desire for truth. Communities must understand this responsibility if the public schools are to be allowed to meet this goal.

3. Participation by citizens is a necessity. Cooperation between the school and the community can only be attained through meaningful participation by both groups. Lay citizens must be involved in the planning, policy-making, problem-solving, and evaluation of the school. The public school must maintain close ties with the community if it is to remain relevant to life.

4. Two-way communications are essential. If people in a community are to share in the educational enterprise, they must have adequate information on which to base their decisions. If the school is going to meet the educational needs of the community, it must be sensitive to the community's goals, concerns, aspirations, and needs.

Do these four principles sound familiar? Would it be possible to change a few words and change these four principles from basic ingredients within a good school-relations program to basic ingredients within a good Community Education plan?

In reading the printed materials now available on school public relations, one is continually impressed with the similarity between what public relations men consider good public relations and what community educators consider good education.

---

[2] Ibid. pp. 148-164.

Community Education: From Program to Process

It would be easy, then, to draw the conclusion that Community Education is, in reality, a good public relations program and community educators are basically public relations directors. Part of this conclusion seems justified. However, it is not valid. While good Community Education does assure good public relations, the purposes of Community Education are quite separate from those of public relations. Community educators believe that Community Education is good education—that for our educational system to survive and prosper citizens must be involved in its growth and development. The basic similarity between community educators and public relations directors is that both recognize the fact that good education assures good public relations. Public relations people have recognized that some of the essential principles underlying good education revolve around positive community participation, and that quality education is much easier to sell than ineffective, irrelevant education. Community educators recognize the development of this quality education as their job. Public relation directors see their role as advertising its existence.

The basic point to be made here is that the community educator has the basic ingredients for good public relations at his fingertips. The basic purpose of his position is to establish the quality educational program that public relations people believe essential to any good public relations program.

The Do's and Don'ts of Telling Your Story

Since the basic ingredients for good public relations already exist in Community Education (quality education), it now becomes essential to discuss how the public can be made aware of the very positive aspects of their educational program. The remainder of this chapter will deal with establishing some objectives and guidelines for communicating the school story and some specific techniques to consider for use in this report. Since the entire context of the book deals with the "listening" and communicating aspect of community development, we will cover only the "telling" side of public relations in this section.

There are several do's and don'ts applicable to any presentation made by an educator. The do's provide many basic rules that should be observed.

Do: Attempt to provide all information about schools and education to the community. This should be done on a continuous basis, rather than sporadically.

Do: Attempt to collect and analyze as much information as you can about the community you are serving. This not only assists you in determining what information is meaningful to the community, it also assists you in providing the educational system with necessary feedback. This input stage is of great assistance in evaluating the impact of specific educational programs upon the community.

Do: Attempt to stress the importance of education to the well-being of the entire society in everything that you do.

Do: Attempt to establish a strong base of community support through your programs and presentations. This support, once established, must be carefully maintained and nurtured.

Do: Attempt to develop within the community a feeling of partnership with the school—a feeling that education is a joint undertaking and that both the school and the community share in a commonality of purpose.

With any listing of items that should be observed and recognized, there are always things that should be avoided.

Don't: Sell the citizenry short in terms of their ability to understand complex educational problems and issues.

Don't: Attempt to gain public support through exaggerated promises or concerns. Information should be presented as objectively as possible.

Don't: Continually bother the media with stories that are of little interest to people outside the educational system. Attempt to establish a relationship of mutual respect with the media, so that when you tell them you have something of interest for them, they will believe you.

Don't: Present anything to the media or to the public that is not well-thought-out, well-documented, and well-timed.

Don't: Attempt to present raw data—just facts and figures. Interpret what these facts and figures mean clearly and concisely, in as objective a manner as possible.

Don't: Establish a presentation for the general community. Have a specific audience in mind when preparing any communication and plan the communique for that audience.

Don't: Be disappointed when after all of your efforts there are still people who feel that the schools waste money, are negligent, and are a failure. You will never convince all people that public education, no matter how good, is good enough.

With these basic guidelines, let us now turn our attention to some specific ways public relations people reach their audience. The discussion will be divided into two parts: personal contact and mass media. It is important to recognize at the outset that it is impossible to suggest a "best" means of communication. This must be done locally by people knowledgeable about the community and the techniques available. Some of the means of transmitting information that will be discussed will be very appropriate for a community educator's use in one circumstance, totally impractical and inappropriate in others. The decision as to whether a communication technique is appropriate or not must be made locally based upon two things:

1. Knowledge of the community

2. Knowing the group with which you are attempting to communicate.

Personal Contact

Personal contact is certainly the most effective means of communicating with the public, and the most effective form of personal contact is face-to-face, person-to-person conversation. The problem presented by this and any other personal contact from that is selected (face-to-face, small group discussion, telephone conversations, or individual letters,) is that extensive time and money must be expended for any large scale program. The advantages of this type of program are numerous, however. In addition to its high rate of effectiveness, personal contact allows for the clarification of any misunderstanding that might arise. Questions, concerns and misinterpretations can be discussed and clarified. The community educator is given a chance to appraise reactions to a proposed plan or specific program that is discussed, providing an informal evaluation that allows him to establish a "feel" for the community. Personal contacts allow the citizen an opportunity to see educators and school personnel as real people — as warm, friendly, concerned individuals who have a sense of purpose and a desire to make education all that it should be. This feeling provides a positive context for the information that is being presented.

Since personal contact techniques are so expensive and time consuming, they must be utilized with great discretion, being used only when mass forms of communication will not serve the same purpose. If some form of personal contact is decided upon, the decision then must be made as to which type will bring the greatest return in terms of time and money expended, and people effectively reached. If a telephone call, for example, will serve basically the same purpose as a personal visit, little would be gained by expending additional time and money for a one-to-one meeting.

The following general guidelines are an attempt to assist a community educator in deciding which form of personal contact to use. Again, they are not intended to be universal rules and certainly should be modified to fit existing local circumstances.

Face-To-Face and One-To-One

This form of communication is both the most expensive and the most effective when used appropriately. In considering the use of face-to-face communication, it is important to think through your purpose of communicating. If it is to disseminate information only, or to get specific information from the community, other techniques would probably be as effective and could be done with less expenditure of energy. Face-to-face communication should only be considered when the group you are attempting to reach has been somewhat defined and determined, and when there is a reason to believe that what you are trying to communicate will be misinterpreted unless there is a chance to discuss these misinterpretations immediately. Using face-to-face communications is further advisable when it is quite possible that mistrust exists between the school and the group to be contacted, or when immediate feedback from the community is specifically desired. There are several examples where schools have selected a face-to-face communication approach and have had great success.

Adult basic education (Chapter 5 discussed this in greater detail) is a program that public schools have accepted as a part of their total program where their most effective recruitment is through face-to-face communication. Adult basic education students are a legally well-defined group of people. They might easily misinterpret information that they have no chance to question and discuss, and they often have little or no trust in the public schools. Further, it has been proven that mass communication techniques are very inappropriate and unsuccessful with this group. In terms of our previous discussion concerning the determination of groups that require face-to-face contact, this group is certainly appropriate.

There are many other situations that legitimately require face-to-face communication: establishing groups of people that might be interested in community problem solving; reaching senior citizens to involve them in the educational program or in educational planning; attempting to get numerous community agencies involved in a unified effort; attempting to establish groups of teen-agers for service oriented projects that benefit the community. The list could continue, but the point is this—you must decide if a given situation requires a face-to-face contact, with an accompanying extensive expenditure of time and money, or if it can be handled in some other way.

Telephone Communications

Telephone communication as a means of personal contact provides many of the advantages of face-to-face communication and greatly reduces the amount of time required to accomplish the purpose of the contact. The telephone allows for discussion, questions and answers, and feedback to the communicator. It is not conducive, however, to establishing feelings of warmth and concern. The nonverbal clues that often assist us in a face-to-face conversation are lacking over the telephone than in personal conversation. The telephone is excellent, however, when you want to collect specific information, remind a group of something, or discuss programs or concerns with an individual who would be relatively receptive to you and to education generally.

Small Group Discussions

Small group discussions, as provided through coffee klatsches, etc., present many of the same opportunities that the one-to-one approaches do, while at the same time providing a great conservation of energy. While individual personal concerns are not normally brought out as well in these small group sessions, lively discussions can occur and positive feelings can be established between the community educator and members of the group. Furthermore, feedback can be achieved almost as well as in the one-to-one technique. This procedure is often ignored because of the effort required to set up the meetings. Educators should take a tip from politicians who use this technique frequently and find that the time and effort required to establish the meeting is certainly well-expanded.

Letter Writing

While some letter writing must be included under the mass media section, personal letters should be included as forms of personal contact. Personal letters do allow an individual to express warmth and friendship and to communicate specific information quite effectively. Further, a well written letter can overcome hostile or somewhat negative feelings and concerns. The great disadvantage is the elimination of feedback. There are few opportunities for the letter writer to ever know how the letter really affected the person written to and whether the desired effect was achieved or not. Letters should generally be used to convey appreciation, to develop good will, and to convey information. Personal letters can be developed to be sent to many individuals with little or no change in the body of the letter. This can normally be accomplished by defining the group of people to receive the letter to a limited interest group and then addressing the body of the letter, specifically to that interest. If the letter is to be personal, however, each letter must be individually typed and signed. Addresses with "Resident" and "Boxholder" should be avoided.

An example of proper use of the personal letter technique was demonstrated by a community educator establishing a high school program for adult students. By studying old school records and other available data he developed a list of non-high school graduates in the community. He then composed a letter of invitation and had each personally addressed, typed, and signed. The letter was developed around the common need of each – the need for a high school education.

Personal contact in any of the forms discussed is desirable and certainly preferred over mass communication techniques. It is simply impossible, however, to utilize only personal contact techniques and still reach the extensive numbers of people within the area served by any community educator. Necessary time and resources simply are not available and this requires the community educator to look for other means of communicating with the public.

Using Mass Media

Knowing how to use the mass media well is an important tool to the community educator. As previously indicated, personal contact is superior to the mass media, but is impractical for communicating with the general public. Mass media can be effective and, if used properly, can communicate an intended message to literally thousands of people at a relatively low cost. The problem is that most educators are not trained in the utilization of mass media and, as a result, do not achieve maximum value from their expenditure.

To initiate a discussion on proper utilization of mass media, Sumption and Engstrom provide some general principles governing the selection and use of communication media that are excellent.

"1. Identify and catalog all available media.

2. Develop long-range plans for the utilization of the most promising media.

3. Choose the medium or media best adapted to the time, the message, and the coverage desired.

4. As far as possible, develop a balanced usage of available media.

5. Establish and maintain a fair and equitable policy for news releases.

6. If possible, make use of all available media over a period of time.

7. Utilize media in such a way as to involve a maximum number of people in the transmission of messages as long as it does not detract from the effectiveness of the message.

Public Relations and Community Education

8. Other factors being equal, select the media which requires the least time and effort to encode the message since facility or preparation is important.

9. Encode the message to suit the medium to be used in order to achieve maximum effectiveness.

10. Maintain a close professional relationship with those in charge of community-based media, and respect requirements as to form, space, accuracy, and deadlines.

11. Accord public recognition to media and individuals who have made special contributions or rendered outstanding service to school-community communication.

12. Conduct periodic evaluations of the adequacy, appropriateness, and effectiveness of the media used." [3]

Each of these basic guidelines, if studied and integrated into a communications program, will greatly assist in enhancing the quality of a mass media program.

While there are many forms of mass media, the remainder of this discussion will focus on five basic areas: newspapers, radio, television, school publications, and mass communication letter

Newspapers

Communicating with the public through newspapers may take several different forms: paid and public service advertisements, regular news articles, editorials, and letters to the editor. Using all forms of expression available through this media greatly enhances the community educator's chances of gaining maximum value from community newspapers.

To begin, any new community educator should get to know his local newspaper and its staff. Try to find out what the paper stands for,

---

[3] Ibid. p. 145.

community positions it has taken in the past, and the general stance that has been taken toward education generally and Community Education in particular. Find out what the newspaper's policy is on printing school news articles, on providing space for special pictorial pages, and on giving space or special rates for school advertising. Learn what the paper's deadline dates are and days of the week or seasons of the year when news is appreciated more than others. Gloria Dapper in her book entitled *Public Relations for Educators,* states that as a rule of thumb, newspapers attempt to balance their advertising and news on a 60-40 percent basis — 60 percent advertising and 40 percent news. On days when advertising is heavy, additional news stories are desired. [4]

Get to know the editor and the reporters assigned to cover education. Try to establish some positive relationships of mutual trust. Newspaper men and educators have frequently been at odds, with educators perceiving news reporters as threatening the position of the school. This position hardly seems justified in light of the overwhelming support that newspapers usually accord public schools in millage elections.

While newspapers may periodically report negative and inaccurate information about schools, by getting to know newspaper people and establishing a bond of trust and friendship, a much better position is established to get positive information to the press regularly and to reduce the effect of some of the negative news that might be printed.

One community educator even recruited the editor of a large urban newspaper to teach a course in "Public Issues" in the adult evening program. Not only did he get an outstanding teacher, but a convert to the program he was attempting to sell as well.

In addition to the editor and education reporter, there is another person who is important to the community educator on the newspaper — the advertising layout man. This is the person who designs and

---

[4] Gloria Dapper, *Public Relations for Educators,* The Macmillan Company, New York, 1964, p. 52.

lays out advertisements for the newspaper and prepares them for print. He can be of invaluable assistance to a community educator in preparing advertisements for his programs. All too often, community educators' attempts to lay out ads to be placed in the paper are amateurish and non-descript. People who do not have an artistic or design background should recognize that there is a special skill involved in making an eye-catching and attractive advertisement. The layout man, if given the basic information necessary, and a free hand, can make an advertisement stand out from the print around it and draw people's attention to his message.

In developing a newspaper advertisement, it is also important to realize that large amounts of print must be broken by pictures or drawings, and that if one attempts to get by with minimum size ads filled only with printed information, very few people will notice them. While it costs more to purchase a large advertisement that catches the eye, the increased number of people that read it more than justifies the increased cost.

The timing for an advertisement is also crucial, especially advertisements for Community Education programs. This is true because consideration has to be given for registration. Normally, the ad should appear three to five days prior to the opening of class registration, with short reminder ads just prior to and through the registration period. In planning your newspaper advertising program, it might be of mutual benefit to you and other community organizations to plan an ad jointly and share the cost. This reduces the advertising expenditure for each agency and allows the total ad to be larger and more eye-catching.

The third way to use a newspaper effectively is to gain editorial support for specific projects or educational plans. The editorial page allows a newspaper to present an opinion based upon facts. An opinion supporting a specific program or project of a community educator is of immense value and it costs nothing. If the community educator has laid his ground work well and has established proper relationships with the newspaper personnel, editorial support is possible.

On the same page with the editorial, one normally finds the "Letters to the Editor" feature. These letters supporting Community Education are of great assistance to a program. This is especially true because of the large percentage of newspaper readers who read these letters. While it is possible for the director himself to write letters to the editor, it is much more effective when others who are not employed by the educational system submit their opinions. During the course of a year, Community Education directors receive many offers for assistance or queries as to what an individual might do to support the program. A specific suggestion that they put their views in a letter to the editor might be of great assistance.

Radio

Radio remains an extremely effective communication media. It has not been replaced by television. Radio is growing yearly and is a very healthy, dynamic industry. It should not be overlooked as an excellent vehicle for mass communication and as a necessary ingredient within a total public relations program. Radio can serve two primary purposes: it can be used to air educational programs of special interest to the listening public, and it can be used as an advertising medium to promote special educational programs or projects. To get the most for your dollars and time, there are several important things you should consider.

When considering the establishment of an educational radio program, many educators become excited about the possibilities inherent in radio programming without considering the realities of time and effort required to produce a good program. In many smaller communities, especially, it is quite possible for an educator to request and be given a weekly radio program. While the possibilities of such an arrangement are exciting, it is quite possible that inexperience and lack of sufficient planning time will turn this weekly program into a boring, deadly weekly session that no one is willing to listen to. The image of education that is presented if this occurs is the image that educators should avoid at all cost. Producing a radio program or weekly series of programs just because the time is available will do more damage than completely avoiding radio programming entirely.

If you have a very definite idea for a radio program that you think would be stimulating and exciting, and if you are willing to spend the hours required to carefully plan for the program or weekly series, you should then consider requesting some time spots from the radio station. Once you have accepted the responsibility, you should work closely with the radio station producer to assess and evaluate the programs that are presented and continually try to improve the programming quality.

Planning for radio advertisements is quite different. As an advertising media, radio provides instant communication with a very large audience. The size of the audience varies throughout the day. Radio stations realize this and establish their advertising rates to reflect the size of the listening audience. Prime time rates carry the highest advertising cost because the advertisements are aired during the peak listening hours. The lowest advertising rates are those established for the times when the listening audience is the smallest.

Many community educators, when considering radio advertising, consider using only that time available through radio stations that is granted free for public service purposes. While public service advertisements do provide a means of communicating over radio, it must be understood that these ads are aired at those times when the listening audience is the smallest. This is in no way a negative reflection on radio stations. They make money only by selling advertising time and they simply cannot afford to give away prime time.

The community educator must accept this and decide whether or not his purposes are being met through public service time only. In most cases, they will not be. If the primary purpose to be served is mass communication with as many people as possible, prime advertising time seems crucial.

Understanding this, the community educator can work out a variety of combinations of time and advertising rates. Most radio stations will reduce rates at prime time periods for educators or give some prime time free for each ad purchased. Specific rates and arrangements can be worked out to fit the needs of the radio station and the community educator.

It must also be understood that each radio station programs for specific audiences and the community educator must know what audience he is attempting to reach before contracting with any radio station. While it is important that radio advertising be shared among local radio stations, it is not wise to contract with all local radio stations for all advertising. It would be unwise, for example, to advertise a new program designed for the elderly on a radio station that features rock music; or to advertise a special teen program on a station that specializes in family and religious music. By knowing the audience you wish to reach and the audience the radio station programs for, advertising can be made more effective.

Once the station or stations have been selected, the community educator should meet with one of the station's program and advertising men to work out the radio spot. Here, the expertise of the producer should be of great assistance. The primary responsibility of the community educator should be that of final approval of the ad that is to be broadcast, in terms of desired impact and accuracy of statements within the ad. Other than this, the radio producer should be encouraged to be as innovative as possible.

Radio can be of great assistance, if used properly, and radio advertisements can generate interest and excitement within the community when they are presented well.

Television

Television has the greatest impact potential of any of the mass media systems. It is also the most expensive and most difficult to utilize. Because of this, great care must be exercised when deciding to use television to communicate with a large audience. Often, because of the glamour associated with television, it is selected for a presentation of information that could be better presented through other media. This is especially true when deciding whether to utilize radio or television. In general terms, radio should be used whenever the presentation is of a general discussion nature, when news about the school is to be presented, or when spot announcements are to be made. Television should be saved for those times when it is important to present a concept or an idea; one that can best be demonstrated pictorally or through dramatization.

It is important also to discuss the difference in time required to produce a television program as opposed to a radio program. Television requires substantially more time and the additional time required of a community educator to develop a television program is wasted if the same communication can be achieved by using the radio or newspapers. The additional time and energy required to produce a television program should result in a program that tells a story that could be told effectively no other way.

After the decision has been made to attempt to tell a story through television, the community educator should attempt to specifically define what it is that is to be told and the major points that should be stressed in telling the story. Once this has been determined, the idea should be presented to the producers of the local television station to determine if any interest exists in televising the story and if the idea is feasible. If interest does exist, the planning from this point should be done jointly to assure a proper presentation of the story. This should include determining how the story can be best portrayed visually while maintaining interest and variety. When these basic decisions have been made, the planning must move to a more detailed stage when each sequence is carefully planned out. Once this is done, rehearsal can begin, climaxed by either a live presentation or video-taping.

As indicated previously, television time is expensive and difficult to obtain. Another method of getting television coverage that is less demanding is through news stories. Often television crews are available for programs or presentations of general interest to the community. A well-planned news story can be as effective as a specially prepared television program, it can be obtained free, and it can be accomplished with a minimum of effort. It is important to continually watch for activities and special interest stories in which television news commentators might be interested. By constantly watching for programs of special interest, the amount of television coverage received by a district can be greatly expanded.

School Publications

Still another very effective form of mass communication is the printed materials produced by the school district itself. It usually is distributed to advertise special events, or provide information about the educational program. The degree of influence that can be achieved by these publications is dependent upon the visual impact and the quality of the presentation of information. While expanded visual impact and content·quality require much thought and care, and it is essential that this time is spent, a basic knowledge of printing and advertising techniques is also necessary to achieve the desired response for the least amount of money.

There are a variety of materials prepared and distributed by public schools that serve many different purposes. School newsletters that are sent to parents and community residents are usually designed to describe the educational program in rather positive terms, or to explain educational issues or problems faced by the school. Brochures are often developed to explain a specific program or project within the educational system, or to advertise the availability of special programs and opportunities. Leaflets and pamphlets are normally designed to describe a forthcoming event or to encourage participation in a school-sponsored activity. Each unique type of school publication fulfills its own specified purposes, and the type of publication that should be used can only be determined by the local community educator. The decision as to what form the publication should take must be based on local purposes to be accomplished, publications already in existence, and the extent of available funds for the purpose.

Regardless of the type of publications to be developed, there are certain basic commonalities that affect all publications that should be incorporated into the publication planning:

1. *Establishing the purpose for publishing*
    It seems quite evident that publications should not be developed, printed and distributed without a reason. It is an unfortunate fact, however, that this happens frequently. Among community educators, it seems that the thing to do in advertising adult course offerings, for example, is to produce a brochure which describes the courses available and explains where and when registration takes place. It is done primarily because everyone else seems to be producing brochures rather than because it is an effective recruiting technique. Prior to committing oneself to any publication, a decision must be made concerning the basic purpose to be achieved, the audience with whom you wish to communicate, and the way this can best be accomplished while maintaining a balanced cost-effectiveness ratio. Once these considerations have been thought out, it is then possible to select the best publication vehicle.

2. *Layout and Design*
    Once the purpose of a publication has been established, the basic layout and design must be considered. While this is usually done most effectively by professionals, basic ideas can be established

and graphically presented by the community educator. In most instances, the layout of the publication should be developed first and the written text adapted to this layout. This is done primarily because of budget restrictions which limit the size of the publication to be a specified number of pages. All layout should be developed on the same size paper that will be used in the publication to establish a feeling for the impact that will be made. In determining what size paper should be used, it might be helpful to determine the size of the paper the printer has in stock. If it is possible to develop a publication that can be cut in even multiples of standard paper stock, paper waste can be eliminated, thus reducing total cost. In planning the layout, test all folds and staples that will be in the publication to be sure they do not cut across a picture, a diagram, or an important part of the text. Finally, when laying out the publication, attempt to establish a balanced-looking page. Too many pictures on one portion of the page or an inappropriate use of different type size often destroys the attractiveness of the publication.

3. *Establishing an Appropriate Text*
   The text obviously must be based upon the predetermined purpose for the publication. In very general terms, it should correspond closely to any pictures or illustrations, should clearly state the desired message, and should be as brief as possible while still expressing the intended message. Educators are often guilty of using more words than are necessary. Attempt to provide variety in the writing by using different sentence lengths, varying paragraph size, and varying word choice. Also, because educators are fond of large words when small ones suffice, a word of warning should be given, encouraging the use of simple, direct words whenever possible.

4. *Printing*
   Prior to preparing anything for printing, the community educator should contact several printing companies and establish a working relationship with the one that can provide both effective assistance and competitive rates. Once the printer has been selected, he can be of great assistance in selecting paper color and quality, size type to be used, color of ink, and different techniques for saving money, while maintaining appropriate printing quality.

While a good printer is the best person to advise you on specifics, some general information might be helpful:

a. In selecting paper, coated paper (the shiny kind) usually assures the clearest pictures, but is more expensive and the print often is more difficult to read because the paper reflects light. Dull paper is less expensive and the print on it is easier to read.

b. In selecting color, it might be possible to get a better price on one particular color the printer might have overstocked.

c. Do not attempt to save money by reducing type size and getting more words on a page. This merely discourages people from reading publications.

d. Always attempt to use high quality photographs and professional illustrations. The printer can assist you in determining which type of photograph is best for printing purposes.

e. In selecting a printer, look for someone who can do the total job. Often this includes collating pages after they are printed, and binding them. Whatever the total job is, make sure the printer is set up to handle it.

f. Attempt to give the printer as much time as possible. This allows him to give you a quality job and often avoids the additional costs that might be incurred if he is required to pay overtime rates to finish your publication.

5. *Proofreading and Final Approval*
    During the rush of getting materials printed, proof-reading is often ignored. This is a mistake. While it is true that a good printer proofreads his work before printing, it is equally true that the community educator is the person who knows best what he is trying to communicate and how he wants it presented. In the final analysis, the responsibility for quality falls upon the community educator, not the printer. At this point, it would be unfortunate

Public Relations and Community Education

to publish something with one or two errors because time could not be spared to assure a corrected final product.

School publications can be an effective tool, but must be well-thought-out and well-designed if they are to be effective.

Mass Communication Letters

The mass-mailed letter, when well-developed and thoughtout, can become a personalized and effective means of communicating a message to a specific group within the community. There are three different ways that mass-mailed letters can be used effectively:

1. A letter can tell a story, describing a program presently in operation or one that is being planned. It can be used to keep a community informed of a variety of educational activities provided through the school.

2. It can be used as a reminder of forthcoming programs, activities, or existing services offered by the educational system.

3. It can be used as a means of persuading an individual to accept a certain point of view, or to do something that he otherwise might not do. This is often evidenced in letters from community educators requesting millage support, or to get adults to enroll in some of the adult courses available through the schools.

Making these kinds of mass-mailings work requires adherance to certain rules. In general, any mass communication letter should be presented very briefly and very concisely. The first two or three sentences should catch the reader's eye and interest, and get him immediately into the body of the letter. Often, if interest cannot be obtained in the first few sentences, the letter will be thrown away as just another piece of junk mail. The general tone of the letter should be personal and warm, directed to the needs or interests of the recipient. An attempt should be made at friendliness in the letter similar to the tone that would be used when writing to an acquaintance who is not a close friend. An attempt should be made to achieve warmth while maintaining an acceptable distance. Throughout the letter, it is important to continually attempt to achieve variety, both in word choice and sentence lengths, and to avoid using cliches, overused words, and educational jargon.

Often, a P.S. at the end of a letter (handwritten if possible) attracts additional attention and can present one final, important statement.

Once the letter is written, it is important to get a reaction to it. Select one or two people whom it is believed are good writers and who will give an honest reaction. Find out what they think the letter is saying, what they feel its general impact is, and if there is anything confusing or unsaid.

Once this is complete, a final editing should be done. This should be done by asking several questions:

1. Is the overall impact of the letter a positive one?
2. Is the letter grammatically correct and are all words spelled correctly?
3. Does it say what was intended in a manner that is pleasing and eye-catching?
4. Do the first few sentences create interest in reading further?
5. If any response is required or desired, is it clearly stated where and how this response should be made?

Once the final editing has been completed, the letter is ready for printing and mailing. A check with the post office regarding their mailing regulations might avoid possible problems when the material is ready to mail. Be sure that it is known what mailing rates are available for the type of mailing being planned. Once this has been done, the printing and mailing can then be completed.

Summary

In an article entitled, "Pitfalls in School Public Relations," the problems of underestimation in public relations are described. [5]

---

[5] "Pitfalls in School Public Relations," from *Public Relations Gold Mine,* Vol. 7, published by National Public Relations Association of the National Educational Association, 1965, 1201 Sixteenth Street, Washington, D.C., pp. 5-14.

Educators continually underestimate the scope of the task of public relations; the thinking and planning necessary for a good program; the time and effort required to develop a good newsletter, radio program; or news article; and the ultimate benefits that can accrue to an educational system that does develop a good public relations program.

"There probably is no enterprise in America which depends so much upon the winning of consent from so many groups simply to be able to do a good job."[6]

---

6 Ibid. p. 6.

SECTION IV

Staffing for Community Education

CHAPTER IX

Determining and Meeting Staffing Needs

Community Education will require different staffing than that found in the traditional school. The staffing requirements will fall into three areas — recognition of staffing available in existing agencies outside the school setting; the necessity for modification of the roles now being played by the traditional school staff; and the need to add additional staff members to carry out new responsibilities.

Outside Staffing

One of the facets of a Community Education program is coordination with other agencies and community social activities. In this regard, the staffing of Community Education will include all the staff members of all the governmental units, social agencies, and other groups involved in education. The size of this group will be formidable, and it will require great effort to just identify these people. The number of people involved in the education of adults outside the traditional school is often much larger than most people realize.

Generally, the community school staff will have little input into the selection of the staff of other agencies. The important thing is to be aware of all of these resources and to incorporate them into the total program of Community Education. In addition, it is also important that these people from other agencies recognize the Community Education concept and their part in it. This will be a difficult task to accomplish, and it will take a considerable amount of time. The immediate reaction is often one of mistrust and threat. It will be the responsibility of those building the Community Education program to work with these other groups to define the concept, illustrate its value and involve outside groups in its implementation. At first, it will be necessary to reassure such groups of the need for their services in the total plan. As they become more involved, they will begin to realize that their programs and services actually increase in size and scope and that such coordination is the most appropriate way to attack community problems and improve conditions. Once the initial concept is understood and accepted by such groups, the primary concern becomes one of establishing techniques for cooperation, coordination, and effective communication.

Traditional Staff

The staffing problems affecting the traditional staff relate primarily to the conceptual base on which the staff operates. The roles performed currently by most people in education are an outgrowth of what they believe is their sphere of responsibility. If, for example, a board member or an administrator feels responsibility for only the students in his community of a certain age, then the school program will reflect such responsibility. If the school custodian feels that only certain students are to be in his building, then his attitude and performance will reflect this belief. If a building principal believes that his concerns should not go beyond the school grounds then he will divorce himself from problems outside those boundaries. If a teacher views her primary role as one of instilling the three "R's," then that is the endeavor toward which she will direct most of her efforts.

The point is that the activities of all persons are based upon their perceptions of "this I believe" about their particular jobs. The basic difference between educational personnel in the traditional school (board members, administrators, teachers, auxiliary staff) and a community school will center around the difference in basic philosophy as to the role of the school in education.

Determining and Meeting Staffing Needs

In order to make this point more apparent, we must also look at the difference between what one believes and what one says he believes. If the Community Education concept is compared to the philosophical statements listed by educators, one would find a great deal of similarity. In fact, it might be claimed, with a high degree of legitimacy, that one of the accomplishments of Community Education is that it corrects some of the hypocracies of education.

To illustrate, let us take a look at a few of these hypocracies of educators — those differences between what school people say they believe and how they actually perform.

Belief - The first years of the life of a child are extremely important in the development of attitudes and intelligence.

Hypocrisy - Until recently very few programs were available for children in this age group and even now most of the existing ones are federally funded programs for disadvantaged children. Public support of education at the kindergarten level is just now being instituted in some states and is almost nonexistent on a pre-kindergarten level. In most states, formal learning starts at a specific age, geared to a specific month, a condition which is contrary to most educational evidence related to learning.

Belief - Education is a gestalt with the school being only one of the forces influencing the education of the individual.

Hypocrisy - Most schools operate as though they were the only educative force in the community. Despite the fact that a student spends less than 11 percent of his time each year in the classroom, there is almost no effort to recognize other educational inputs. The relationship between what takes place at home, church or in the neighborhood and the classroom is almost totally ignored. Educators, for example, know that language patterns are almost totally influenced by the home, that success in education is a result of home attitudes toward school, that school work will be affected by such things as diet, rest, health and various trauma outside the school setting. Yet, educators do little or nothing to allow or compensate for such influences. It may be that some students see this more clearly than do the professional educators. "Dad says I can quit school when I'm fifteen, and I am sort of anxious to because there are a lot of things I

Community Education: From Program to Process

want to learn how to do and as my uncle says, I'm not getting any younger." [1]

Belief - Education should be relevant to the society it serves.

Hypocrisy - The curriculum within the schools has moved farther and farther from the purposes it was originally established to serve. When free public education was first begun, it was designed to meet the needs of society. The three "R's" were offered to provide a more literate population for the purposes of employment and citizenship. The professions which were offered—law, medicine, and the clergy,— were aimed at providing the necessary services for the community. Like so many other institutions, the schools have continued to isolate themselves from the communities which they are supposed to serve until they now dispense information without knowledge as to its relevance to the community. The situation might well be described as follows:

"I can solve a quadratic equation,
but I cannot keep my bank balance straight.

I can read Goethe's Faust in the original,
but I cannot ask for a piece of bread in German.

I can name the kings of England since the Wars of the Roses,
but I do not know the qualifications of the candidates in the next election.

I know the economic theories of Malthus and Adam Smith,
but I cannot live within my income.

I can recognize the "leit-motif" of a Wagner Opera,
but I cannot sing in tune.

I can explain the principles of hydraulics,
but I cannot fix a leak in the kitchen faucet.

---

[1] Stephen Corey, "The Poor Scholar's Soliloquy," *Childhood Education,* 20, January, 1944, pp. 219-20.

I can read the plays of Moliere in the original,
but I cannot order a meal in French.

I have studied the psychology of James and Titchener,
but I cannot control my own temper.

I can conjugate Latin verbs,
but I cannot write legibly,

I can recite hundreds of lines of Shakespeare,
but I do not know the Declaration of Independence, Lincoln's Gettysburg Address, or the Twenty-Third Psalm." [2]

Belief - The quality of knowledge is increasing at such an "explosive" level that there is a need for more time to educate children.

Hypocrisy - The length of a school year has gravitated toward the minimal figure. School districts which used to have 195 days of school at a time when 180 days were required by state law have now settled on the 180 day school year as both the maximum and the minimum figure. The hours of the school day have also decreased so that the typical school day is now about six hours in length.

Belief - School buildings represent an expensive investment by the community and should receive maximum use.

Hypocrisy - Despite talk about year-round schools and increased use of facilities, most buildings continue to be used only by the K-12 elements of the community. Through a combination of finances, scheduling and possessiveness, most schools are kept in idleness for about 85 percent of the total clock hours each year.

Belief - Education should reflect the community.

Hypocrisy - The local schools have more and more usurped the rights of community involvement and community control. In fact,

---

[2] Bernadine Freeman, "Is This Education?" *The Educational Forum,* Vol. 15, January, 1951, p. 139.

Community Education: From Program to Process

schools have moved so far away from community that they have actually become the adversaries. Schools have become operative unto themselves so that generally the only contact with the community is an information-giving one. School administrators "tell people about the schools, bring parents into the schools, sell the schools to the people. Very few efforts of a continuing type have been mounted which allow parents . . . . . . opportunities to share their feelings about the schools with school officials. Information flow has been primarily one-way. Legitimate outlets have not been provided for protest or discontent. PTA's and similar organizations have often ruled discussions of local school weaknesses out of bounds in order to perpetuate a peaceful, tranquil, and all-is-well atmosphere. As a consequence, school systems have not had safety valves. There are no designed schemes for absorbing or dealing with pressure; no organized way of facing dissatisfaction. The emphasis has been on how well we are doing as reported and defined only by school people . . . . organizations like PTA's have been co-opted by professionals much too often. PTA's and other symbiotic organizations have paid a high price for being loved by school personnel." [3]

Belief - Education is a lifetime process.

Hypocrisy - Educators tend to limit the goals of education, such as the seven cardinal principles of education, to a specific age group. Public school education is limited to that 20 percent of our population between the ages of five and eighteen. Most other education is on a limited scope with scheduling, facilities and instruction allocated low on the priority list. And although there are statistics to show that there are more people who need high school diplomas outside the schools than in; that there are a substantial number of adults who are either illiterate or functionally illiterate; that there is a greater need for health concerns in the adult population than in the student population; the fact remains that in all educational areas the needs of children not only get top priority but often the traditional program tends to exclude all other educational needs.

---

[3] Luvern Cunningham, *Governing Schools: New Approaches to Old Issues,* Charles Merrill Publishing Co., Columbus, Ohio, 1971, p. 176.

Determining and Meeting Staffing Needs

Thus, if we compare what traditional educators and community educators say they believe, one can see a great deal of similarity, at least as it applies to the traditional educative role of the school. The major difference seems to be that Community Education attempts to develop those aspects of education which traditionalists hypocritically fail to promote.

There is another basic difference, however, related to the "process" element of Community Education. In this area, community educators are suggesting that schools take the responsibility for activities which were formerly held to be outside the realm of the schools. Community educators are saying that schools should be the catalytic institution for bringing about coordination of social and governmental agencies, community organization and community involvement. This concept is being re-enforced across the country by the development of community agents, ombudsmen, and programs by Model Cities, the Urban Coalition, and the Office of Economic Opportunity.

Basically, our communities are developing new expectations about the schools. The first expectation is to carry out their traditional job better in relating curriculum to community, involving community in educational decision-making and opening educational opportunities to all of the members of the community rather than just a selected few. But schools also have the responsibility of establishing a new role. They must be the catalyst in helping the community develop esprit de corps, identify its problems and use its resources to influence the decisions related to these problems. This role implies not only opening its doors, but reaching out to those community members who do not respond to the program aspect of Community Education.

Now, how does all this relate to the role of the regular personnel in the traditional school? Assuming that people perform on the basis of their philosophical beliefs, then a change in beliefs will result in a corresponding change in behavior. If the beliefs of board members, administrators, teachers, and auxiliary personnel are changed so that they include the programs and process of Community Education, and if the hypocrisies are eliminated so that there is consistency between belief and performance, then the roles of all those persons in Community Education will be fairly automatic. For boards and administrators, the transition is one of accepting a wider responsibility

Community Education: From Program to Process

and more staffing – of seeing education in a much wider role. For teachers and auxiliary staff, it is one of placing their function in relation to the whole – of realizing that their duties are not the total educational operation but rather a part of it and that other educational needs have equal demands on finances, facilities and other resources of the community.

Community Education Staff

One of the points about Community Education which should be made clear from the outset is that it will take additional staff to carry on the new functions of the school. To start without this as a basic axiom could be disastrous. There have been many school districts which decided to start Community Education by assigning the responsibilities to existing full-time staff members. The result is that the program is never really able to get underway. Community Education implies an expanded role for the school and the expanded role implies additional staff. Until a district is willing to accept this fact, they should not attempt to implement Community Education.

The key role in the development of Community Education will be that of the Community Education director. He may be called community services director, community agent, community developer, ombudsman or something else, but he is the one who is primarily responsible for the development and implementation of Community Education. He needs administrative support, both morally and financially, and he needs cooperation from community and school personnel, but the success of his efforts will depend more upon his personal qualities than upon any other ingredient. Just as the quality of the teacher will be the most significant factor in the educational outcome of the classroom, the quality of the Community Education director will be the most important factor in the development of Community Education. It is therefore extremely important that great care be taken in the selection of this person.

What characteristics should a Community Education director have? It is probably easiest to decide this by looking at the tasks he must perform. The director will be called upon to relate to varying groups. He will have to maintain good relations with the faculty and to work effectively with the administration. He will need to work directly

Determining and Meeting Staffing Needs

with the custodial staff. His range of programs will require that he work as well with adults as he does with children. His responsibilities will require that he be able to relate to large groups as well as to individuals, to the poor and undereducated as well as the educated and affluent, to the business, industrial and governmental community as well as the educational community.

His personal qualities are very important and are described by W. Fred Totten as follows: "Above all else, the director must be creative and have a warm, outgoing personality. He must like people and be capable of showing compassion without pity. He must be the kind of person to be trusted by people of all ages. He must be free from prejudice with respect to people of any race and/or socio-economic circumstances. Humility and consistency are two essential qualities. The director must be in good emotional and physical health and capable of sustained energy and vigor for long periods of time. Flexibility and adaptability are essential personal qualities. The director should be a good team member and a skillful leader." [4]

The nature of the director's job is extremely varied. He will need to be an organizer in order to develop the community with which he is working. He will have to be task-oriented, carrying out his responsibility, regardless of the time involved or schedule required. He will find himself serving on committees of various kinds, surveying the community, working with other agencies, developing and supervising programs, serving as a resource person to the local school staff, visiting homes, speaking at public meetings, employing staff, developing budgets, seeking funding, and administering programs.

"The community service director is a generalist. He must have a thorough knowledge of and be productive in the areas of curriculum, instruction, and supervision. He must be strong in organizational skills and techniques. Much of his work is administrative in nature. He is also called upon to be a counselor and advise on many occasions. Strength in leadership, communication, and human relations skills is essential to

---

[4] W. Fred Totten, *The Community Services Director,* No. 532, Mott Program, Flint, Michigan, p. 3.

his successful performance. His business is composed of people and helping people solve a great variety of human problems. Hence, he must be able to assess the needs of people; then he must plan, implement, and administer programs of learning to help people fulfill their unmet needs. In doing this, he must develop expertise in approaching nonschool agencies for assistance and in bringing into contact all of the efforts of churches and other organizations and groups to serve the learning needs of people. He must also bring into use the many individuals who can serve as resources for learning. All of the building space and other space in the community that can be used for learning programs must be discovered, and arrangements must be made to use the nonschool house space needed." [5]

No other position is so important to the operation of Community Education as that of director. Regardless of the other inputs, the success or failure of the program will depend upon who fills this position. The combination of personal qualities, training, and experience are the factors to look for in such a person. And while the previous job description and personal characteristics may sound difficult to fulfill, the fact is that literally hundreds of these positions are being filled by persons with energy, ability and dedication who meet the requirements listed.

Teachers

The additional programs related to students and adults will require additional teaching staff. Some of the programs, such as remedial and enrichment classes, high school completion and basic education will require certificated teachers. Other programs relating to avocational interests such as hobbies, recreation and special interest areas will have teachers who have developed these specialties themselves. Other classes in the vocational area will be staffed by people degreed or licensed in that particular area. Persons staffing these positions may be paid or they may be volunteers.

---

[5] Ibid. p. 5.

Supervisors and Assistants

There will be many activities for adults, youth, and children which will require staff in other than a teacher-student relationship. Athletic contests, roller skating, dancing, public meetings, and similar types of activities require staff to accept the responsibility for supervising the activities and provides the services necessary to carry out these aspects of the program. This staff can be solicited from local personnel, either paid or volunteer, through the use of teachers on a part-time basis, and for some activities, the use of students.

Community Workers

Working with the community will require additional staffing. First of all, in order to do the massive job of organizing the community and providing for community involvement it is necessary to have people to do the door-to-door contacting and invest the time necessary for working on community problems.

Secondly, despite all the outstanding characteristics of the director, it is frequently easier to use indigenous personnel for work in the community. This is particularly true if the community being worked with is significantly different from the personal background of the director.

In any event, there is a need for staff to carry out the process aspect of Community Education. As the responsibilities in this area increase, there will be increased need for additional staff to work in the community, either paid or volunteer.

Training

An important part of staffing relates to training. For the traditional school positions, teachers and administrators, it will mean a change in the current training programs. At the university level in both the graduate and undergraduate programs, it is necessary to introduce the concept of Community Education. By influencing the philosophical concepts of those going into the teaching profession, it will make it possible for them to perform in a way which will enhance both the inception and development of Community Education in their districts. For those professionals who have already completed their training, it will be necessary to carry on extensive in-service programs so that they are aware of the Community Education concept. The in-service approach will also be the best technique for having influence on auxiliary staff.

Training of teachers of classes in the Community Education program, will deal primarily with techniques. Teachers employed in these classes are usually well-equipped with regard to the subject matter which they are teaching. The shortcomings are generally in the area of methodology. For those who have never been teachers, there is a need for training in teaching techniques. For those who have been teachers, the problem usually centers around their lack of experience in teaching adults. There are few programs established for dealing with these problems. Some colleges and universities have recognized this need and are attempting to establish such programs. In general, however, the efforts which are being made, are being carried out on a local, school district basis. This whole area is covered more completely in Chapter 10.

The training of supervisors and assistants is an easier matter. The nature of these duties usually are such that training requirements can be handled locally through in-service education. The responsibilities of these jobs are of the nature of opening buildings, providing operational services and interpreting rules and regulations. As such, there is little training needed and usually individuals are able to function in these positions effectively after limited experience.

The training of the Community Education director is the most sensitive part of the training program. As mentioned before, the success or failure of Community Education will be more closely tied up with this individual than with any other person or group of persons. The characteristics to look for in the selection of such a person already have been described. Such characteristics are necessary but not sufficient ingredients in a successful director. In order to get maximum results, there are certain training inputs which are necessary.

There are several training programs which have been tried and have had varying degrees of success. One such program might be classed as a short-term training program. The first step in this program is to identify persons with the proper personal characteristics. The training consists of a short training period of approximately six weeks. The training experience is made up of classes and seminars dealing with the concept, history, implementation, financing and duties related to Community Education, accompanied by an internship experience in Community Education. Variations of this program have consisted of having both the classes and internship carried on over a short period in one community or having a portion of the training, generally the class sessions, at a university, with the additional training spent in an internship in some community.

The common denominator in this training is the feeling that in order for training to be effective it should include an understanding of the concept, information on how to do specific things, and some actual on-the-job experience under a qualified supervisor. The length of the training, as well as the concentration of such training, will depend upon availability of trainees, staff and facilities. There is some evidence to show that short-term training programs are not as effective as longer sessions, but the demands for trained personnel have necessitated more intensive programs of shorter duration. There is also a likelihood that training over a period of time, while directors are performing their jobs, makes the training program more relevant to the trainees' needs, but such a program is only possible when the training program is in proximity to the community of the director.

Another type of training program has been the training program operated by local school districts. This program has been primarily a learning-by-doing program. Trainees become assistants to Community Education directors and go through the process of moving from menial tasks to the more complicated responsibilities of a director. This program has been used primarily by school districts to increase their own programs and replace their personnel. The main problem with such training is that the focus of the program is generally one of observing and copying. Unfortunately, such training programs often result in leaving out the conceptual base of Community Education and the process aspect of operation. As a result, these new directors often fail to understand and promote the total concept, despite their high motivation and good intentions.

A third kind of training deals with university graduate programs. These programs are usually master's degree oriented, although there are some programs at the specialist and even the doctoral level. The offering of such programs has ranged from training programs related to physical education through programs interdisciplinary in nature. Most of these programs, however, are offerings in school administration with Community Education being a specialization in that area, much as one might specialize in elementary or secondary administration.

The placement of such programs in school administration has not been accidental. There is a logic behind why most institutions have moved in this direction in their training.

1. Community Education seems to be most productive when worked through the schools. While this might be the only way in which such a program can be successful, to date it has proved to be the method most likely to succeed. Thus, if the programs are to be run through the school it seems logical to conclude that preparation programs might also be handled by the colleges of education at the higher education level.

2. If one accepts the idea that the school should be the vehicle for implementing Community Education, then there is some advantage to making the director's role administrative. Such a position will give him certain relationships with the school staff, and will allow him to operate on a task-oriented basis without the restrictions of time imposed by the master contract.

3. The career direction of most people in Community Education seems to be toward administration. During the past 35 years, it has been possible to determine from a review of their aspirations, what professional direction community educators will take. While many have stayed in their positions as directors of elementary-size districts, most have gone on to other administrative positions. Some of these positions have been as coordinators of Community Education for the school district, but a large number have moved into more traditional administrative roles such as principalships, central office staff or superintendencies.

4. There is great value in attaching a new role to a traditional discipline. When a new position and new responsibility are identified, it takes some time for it to be accepted or perceived appropriately by other members of the staff. Most new programs and positions have had a difficult and prolonged battle in trying to

receive acceptance by both other educators and the community. By identifying with a traditional discipline, such as school administration, identification, role definition, and acceptance are more immediately accomplished.

5. If the point about identifying with a traditional discipline is accepted, then the only task left is to discover which identification is most appropriate. A close look at the responsibilities of a director of Community Education reveals that he hires and discharges people, builds schedules, arranges for rooms, handles registration, deals primarily in education, must work at public relations, must relate to people of all ages, and does a great deal of administration. The position seems to be more akin to school administration than to any other position.

The graduate training program of community school directors generally consists of core courses, cognate courses in the field of education and electives from areas other than education. The training program will usually be made up of courses in such things as leadership, educational organization, community organization, the conceptual base of Community Education, Community Education administration, adult education, research techniques, and school and community relations. Elective areas, both in and out of education, should be aimed at the development of the individual in areas which will improve his understanding and ability to deal with the individual and the community.

One of the outstanding training programs has been the Mott Inter-University Clinical Preparation Program. This training program was piloted in 1963 and implemented in 1964 and is the outgrowth of coordination and involvement of seven Michigan Universities using Flint, Michigan, as their laboratory. This combination, plus the availability of Mott Foundation dollars, has resulted in a training program which has received national recognition. Approximately seventy interns are selected each year and given a stipend to study in Flint and at a Michigan university for one year. The training is a combination of classes and multiple internships in schools, government and social agencies. The academic portion of the program is composed of classes, seminars and lectures using the Flint staff, the staffs of the seven universities, outside consultants, and speakers brought to Flint from thoughout the country. The nature of this program, and the subsequent placement and accomplishments of the participants, indicates that this program has contributed immeasurably to the training of educational leaders and the promotion of Community Education.

It appears that the need for trained community educators is going to continue to increase. While personal characteristics certainly are of prime importance, our contention is that additional and appropriate training will enhance the individual responsible for Community Education and subsequently enhance Community Education. The programs for training are not all alike and will most certainly change as Community Education becomes more sophisticated. There are, however, some general things which educators currently know about Community Education which should be a part of most training programs. These training aspects should apply in the training of all persons in charge of developing Community Education and whenever certain aspects of the total Community Education process are delegated, should be used in training those assigned persons also.

In general, the most effective type of training appears to be that which includes a mastery of the concept, tools for implementation and an internship under a qualified Community Education director. More specifically, however, a good training program would accomplish the following:

A. *Understanding the Community Education Philosophy:*
1. Each trainee should have established his own philosophy of Community Education and should be able to defend it among his peers.

2. Each trainee should be able to define Community Education and illustrate specific programs and processes by which it is to be implemented.

3. Each trainee should be able to analyze a Community Education program, determine the strengths and weaknesses of the program and determine the extent of community involvement within the program.

4. Each trainee should have achieved a level of competence sophisticated enough to allow him successfully to initiate and operate a Community Education program.

Determining and Meeting Staffing Needs

    5.   Each trainee should understand the Community Education concept well enough to desire to expand this concept wherever he may go, in whatever capacity he may find himself.

B. *Technical Skills for Implementing Community Education:*
1. Each trainee should be able to analyze a community power structure and understand how this power structure can best be utilized for community growth.
2. Each trainee should be able to establish an effective community council.
3. Each trainee should know how to conduct and analyze a community study.
4. Each trainee should understand the relationship that should exist between schools and other community agencies and how to organize these agencies to accomplish the purposes of the Community Education program.
5. Each trainee should be able to initiate and operate specific programs found within the general framework of Community Education — of adult education, recreation, student enrichment, special programs designed to meet special needs, etc.

C. *Humanitarian Concerns Among Interns:*
1. The trainee should be able to describe the complex nature of the society and the resulting effect upon individuals.
2. The trainee should recognize within himself an increased tolerance for human differences and an increased feeling of concern for those within the society.
3. The trainee should understand the shortcomings of our existing education system and should possess a desire to create change within the system.

D. *General Administrative Skills:*
1. The trainee should be able to describe different types of administrative organization and specify where Community Education fits into these structures.
2. The trainee should understand the roles and responsibilities of the superintendent of schools, elementary and secondary

school principals, curriculum directors, school business officials, and other selected administrative personnel.

3. The trainee should understand the basic principles involved in budgeting, decision-making, team management, and current administrative theory.

4. The trainee should understand group processes and know how to lead a group toward goal attainment.

5. The trainee should understand how to create an organizational climate in which all members may make significant contributions.

6. The trainee should be able to communicate orally and in writing with clarity and precision.

CHAPTER X

Establishing an In-Service Program to Meet Staff Needs

In-service education is probably the most maligned, misused, and misunderstood process in education today. At the same time, it potentially is one of the most important tools for change within the educator's "bag of tricks" that is available. Many educators feel that educational goals and objectives can never be truly reached without a vibrant in-service educational process in operation within the educational system.

If change is to take place within a system, it must be done through the people already employed within the system. It is recognized that this usually is difficult, since these same people are usually the ones who created a need for change in the first place. A process for encouraging change and growth must be established to assist individuals in improving their skills and competence.

To state that in-service education is of major importance to community educators is an understatement. To state that Community Education can never reach its true potential without in-service training is redundant. To state that in-service education is normally at best poorly done, and at worst ignored, is stating something everyone knows and accepts.

Community Education: From Program to Process

These statements are all true .... most community educators accept them as fact .... but what is being done to expand insights and to improve the general quality of education? How else can community educators gain commitment to an educational philosophy as demanding and time consuming as the one they espouse, without a sophisticated, comprehensive, and dynamic in-service program?

The basic point is this: While educators recognize all of the negative attributes of existing in-service education, it is simply impossible to develop good Community Education without good in-service, and it is not permissable to allow education to remain in its present unacceptable form.

Educators must recognize that knowledge does become obsolete, that new ideas must be not only learned, but accepted and integrated into our educational philosophies, that people do have to recharge old batteries and be stimulated and excited, and that educators, like all people, lose perspective in their day-to-day routine and must be provided with opportunities to continually reassess and re-evaluate their performance. In-service education can and should provide this.

Establishing a Base for In-Service Education

There seem to be three basic ingredients in the poor programs that educational leaders have attempted to foist upon other educators as in-service training: tradition, noncommitment, and poor financing.

Educators have usually viewed any in-service program as that period of time when they call together a given staff for one or two hours at the beginning of the year to somehow, someway, improve their performance. This is usually done through a speaker of stature making a presentation to a rather large group – a group having mixed emotions as to their presence, the content, and the value of the whole thing.

The rationale for this approach is simple – it is safe and has been done this way for years. There seems to have developed a tacit understanding between the educators planning the in-service and the educators receiving it. If you sit through a rather dull presentation without too many complaints, you won't be expected to change and improve your performance. While this may overstate the case, it is basically true. Information is presented rather traditionally and is seldom internalized by the recipient. When knowledge is not internalized into a basic educational philosophy, it is not used. As a result, little, and usually nothing, results from these attempts.

The second most common reason for failure in in-service programming is noncommitment. In very simple terms, the in-service programs presented suffer from lack of thinking and lack of planning. While most educators stress the importance of in-service education, few are willing to spend the time necessary to make it successful. They ascribe it great importance in words, but not in the amount of time they are willing to spend to assure success. To be meaningful, in-service education must be given a priority of time to assure adequate planning and program development.

The third reason in-service often fails is money. It is continually underfunded. Educators must not only be willing to spend substantial amounts of time in developing a good in-service program, but must be willing to spend the money necessary to see it through as well. In a world of financial priorities, educators seldom give proper priority to the development and growth of the staff that turns ideas into action — the staff that determines the success of the entire program.

As community educators establish a base for a good in-service program, these three negative characteristics must be accounted for. Rather than thinking in negative terms, however, they should be stated positively. In-service education should be designed to insure positive desired change. To do this, adequate time and money must be expended and creative approaches to change should be encouraged and utilized. While this statement attempts to avoid reasons for failure, it does not provide any ideas for assuring success. It cannot be assured that success will be achieved by merely eliminating negative aspects. Positive insurers of success must also be included. Some of these include: involving participants in planning for group and individual differences, establishing objectives, and assuring adequate evaluation.

Planning for Participation

If there is one thing educators have learned from the sociologists and group process people that can assist them in planning in-service education it is the fact that participants must be involved in the total program if they are to gain the most from it. It is important that conclusions reached and plans established in an in-service program emerge from within the group. This insures the product to be a group product and the group then shares in the responsibility of success or failure in the decision. By establishing a program that insures maximum participation of the people that will be involved, greater chances of success are assured.

Recognizing Unique Group Differences

In planning any in-service effort, the group that will be involved must be assessed. Programs should be geared around the group's unique problems and needs and around the concerns common to the group. Programming must start where the group is and move toward the desired goal. It would be wise, for example, to consider whether or not the members of the group know each other. If they do not, it is necessary to get them to know each other well enough to participate effectively in the program that has been planned. If they do know each other, what is the relationship among members of the group? Are they friendly or do they have negative feelings about each other; are they indifferent?

Another concern that might be considered in terms of the group is gearing the in-service program to the level of sophistication of the group members. Determining this general level of sophistication and how much difference there is between members of the group are but two considerations of many that must be accounted for in recognizing the unique differences in groups.

Establishing Objectives and Direction

No in-service program can function effectively without a clear understanding of the program's objectives and the direction that should be taken to reach these objectives. As indicated previously, these objectives and the direction to be taken should be understood by as many people who will be involved in the program as possible. It is fruitless to begin an in-service program with specified goals and objectives if they are not understood or accepted by those partici-

Establishing an In-Service Program to Meet Staff Needs

pating. This step must be accomplished first, before any attempt can be made toward accomplishing the objectives specified.

Evaluation

The importance of establishing in-service education as a priority (both in time and money) has been previously discussed. Placing priority on in-service education requires the inclusion of another element — that of evaluating the product. Whenever we begin discussing extensive time commitments in planning and extensive financial commitments to carry out such plans, we must also discuss a means of determining whether or not it was all worthwhile. This, then, is the evaluation process: This phase, like each of the others should be established jointly and accepted by the entire group involved. The group should participate in establishing what the evaluation criteria should be, and how the evaluation can best be used for improvement and attainment of the pre-established goals. Evaluation is discussed in greater depth in Chapter 15.

Developing the In-Service Program

Developing an in-service program is quite different from planning for an in-service training session. The in-service program entails the total plan developed for the entire year, which will include a variety of activities and training session within it. Planning this total program requires much thought and discussion. To begin, it is important to get rid of the old notion that in-service education always centers around meetings and group get-togethers. Much effective in-service education can be handled through subscriptions to appropriate journals, establishing a regular means of communication such as a newsletter, suggesting specific reading, or developing a professional library that is easily accessible to the staff. Even within the standard concept of in-service education (meeting) there is much room for innovation. Instead of the traditional lecture or lecture-discussion, meetings can be developed around simulation games, the case study technique, two or three day retreats, or a free-wheeling, totally unstructured session inviting people to brainstorm on a given problem or issue.

These suggestions are not intended to be all inclusive, but rather to initiate some thinking and present some creative possibilities for

Community Education: From Program to Process

in-service education. The community educator, in planning an in-service program must consider as many techniques and innovations as possible and determine which ones, or which combination, best fit the training needs of the staff he intends to work with.

The establishment of a good in-service educational program seems to fall naturally into six basic areas:

1. Defining the problem to be attacked.

2. Determining what can be accomplished through in-service training.

3. Establishing general goals and objectives for the in-service effort.

4. Determining how the goals and objectives can best be reached (problem planning).

5. Carrying the program out as planned.

6. Evaluating.

It has been previously stated that inclusion of participants from the beginning is essential. It is restated here to underscore its importance. Participation by those who will be involved is essential for a truly effective in-service effort. This involvement should start at the very beginning with the determination of what is to be achieved through the program. While it is impossible to include all participants in the planning, it is possible to attempt to select a diverse a group as possible to assure incorporating many different and unique ideas and attitudes into the planning. This is often avoided in the interest of expediency and individuals are selected who tend to agree with one another and who can complete the task quickly. Selections of this kind are little better than having no group participation at all, because diverse opinions are never heard.

Defining the Problem to be Attacked

Once the task force that will assist in planning has been determined, they should be asked to define the general problem that

Establishing an In-Service Program to Meet Staff Needs

they should be concerned with. At this point, the community educator should express his specific purposes and provide committee members with any supplemental materials that might assist them. A new director of Community Education, for example, might explain that his purpose for providing in-service education the first year is to establish Community Education in the system as a bona fide part of education, and to make sure that there is general understanding as to what Community Education is, he might present research findings and other information that support the concept of Community Education. This process allows the committee to think through the general purposes of the in-service effort and to redefine these purposes into more meaningful terms for them.

Determining What can be Accomplished Through In-Service

As the committee begins to study the problem, it will become evident that some of the purposes discussed will not be met through in-service alone. Such purposes should be identified so that the committee eliminates discussion of general educational issues and considers only those issues relevant to the proposed in-service training effort. It is necessary to remember at this point that the committee is not rejecting some of the existing educational concerns because they are unimportant, but rather because they cannot be best achieved through the planned in-service. This redefining and narrowing of scope assists the director in determining which general purposes that have been established must be accomplished through other means.

Establishing General Goals and Objectives for the In-Service Education Effort

Once general consensus has been reached as to the general purposes of the in-service efforts, specific objectives should be established. The objectives should be stated in behavioral terms, so that an evaluation can be made upon the completion of the program.

At this point, for example, the committee might determine that since a general goal of the program is the establishment of Community Education as a bona fide part of the system, the specific behavioral objective might be: A minimum of 80 percent of all teachers and administrative personnel participating in the in-service program shall feel strongly enough about the value of Community Education that they will sign a prepared statement to this effect at the conclusion of the program, and the statement will be submitted to the superintendent of schools.

The objective is measurable and can be evaluated at the end of the program. Other factors that might be in an in-service program designed to initiate Community Education might include the upgrading of teachers in specific program areas (such as adult education, recreation, or student enrichment) the reconsideration of existing school system priorities, or the rethinking of custodial job descriptions. Whatever the committee decides, they should attempt to put their thinking into measurable behavioral objectives. If time is a problem it might be possible for the director to assist the committee by taking their generalized goals and writing the initial drafts for the behavioral objectives. The committee can then take these and rewrite and rework them until they are satisfied.

Determining how Goals and Objectives can Best be Reached (Program Planning)

Once goals and objectives have been established, the committee must turn to the problem of planning the in-service program that will best meet these objectives. At this point, the community educator can be of great assistance by providing the group with information concerning a variety of possible techniques they might try that have been successful elsewhere. He should also present what is known about what makes a success in an in-service program to assure the incorporation of concepts that have previously proven to be ingredients of success.

Carrying the Program out as Planned

While this step seems quite evident, it is important to stress the need to carry the program out *as it was planned.* It has happened too often in the past that directors become involved with a variety of other

Establishing an In-Service Program to Meet Staff Needs

activities and forget responsibilities they had assumed, or some of the specific plans of the committee. Whenever group process is used in planning, it is essential that the intent of the group be carried out. Failure to do this is often interpreted as the administrator's attempt to get his own way rather than act on the advice of the committee. At this point, group process begins to disintegrate.

Evaluating

Assuming that the previous steps have been carried out, the evaluation process is a rather simple one. The behavioral objectives must be evaluated at the completion of the program to determine whether or not they were met. If they were not met, some assessment must be made as to why they were not, and a decision then made as to what must be done to see that they are met. This phase also provides some information to assist in future decision-making concerning the value of in-service effort and the extent of funding that it should receive.

A Word About Sensitivity Training

Some approaches being used more and more frequently to achieve staff growth and development center around psycho-process groups, more commonly referred to as sensitivity groups, T. groups, attack or encounter groups, and marathons. This type of training has established a mystique in the educational world and has almost become a cult. You are either "with it" if you have experienced the opportunity to become "sensitized" or "out of it" if you have not.

The basic point that must be made is not that there is anything inherently evil or good in this process, but that it is quite possible to misuse these techniques and establish a sensitivity program because it is the thing to do, rather than because it fits your purposes.

Psycho-process groups are designed to reorganize an individual's basic personality. In reality, they are an off-shoot of group therapy and group counseling. Unless the purpose in your in-service program is the basic modification and reorganization of the personalities of the people that will be involved in the in-service effort, group process of this type should be avoided. Psycho-process groups are extremely dangerous when misused or handled incorrectly.

Community Education: From Program to Process

Summary

The preceding suggestions seem consistent with several national trends in in-service education presented in a recent N.E.A. Research Bulletin:

> "Teachers or their representatives are usually involved in planning the in-service program. Administrators, supervisors, and teachers work as a team.
>
> Greater use is being made of the professional staff within a school system. Non-college credit programs are conducted by school personnel.
>
> School systems are offering a wider variety of opportunities and activities for professional growth in in-service.
>
> School systems are providing more released time during the regular school session for in-service activities.
>
> Compensation is being given for time contributed to in-service education by the teacher outside regular school hours.
>
> School systems are extending the period of teacher employment; the additional time is used for in-service education.
>
> Salary practices recognize experience and preparation.
>
> In-service programs are receiving financial support from sources other than the school system.
>
> Nearly all in-service programs have subjective evaluation; systematic statistical evaluations are not widespread." [1]

---

[1] "Professional Growth of Teachers in Service," *NEA Research Bulletin,* XLV, March, 1967, pp. 25-26.

Establishing an In-Service Program to Meet Staff Needs

Planning for Community Education In-Service

The preceding pages have been directed to a general discussion of in-service education. The information presented provides some broad guidelines for the community educator or any other educator as he plans an in-service effort for his school system.

While these general guidelines present some concerns that all educators must face in planning in-service education, there are specific concerns that also must be considered planning an in-service effort in Community Education.

1. Promoting a new philosophy – The community educator must understand from the outset, that in-service success in Community Education will be more difficult to achieve than in most other areas of education. Most in-service efforts are geared to solving a specific school problem, to the development and utilization of a new technique, or to the stimulation of teachers to encourage a greater teaching effort. While these efforts are often challenging, they usually do not require major philosophical belief changes. Community Education presents a concept substantially different from that held by most educators and community members. To succeed in an in-service effort in Community Education, old belief systems and operational patterns must be broken down before new ones can be developed. It is always difficult to change existing patterns of behavior. Community Education requires this change before success can be achieved.

2. Most educational in-service effort attempts to change people whose lives are dedicated toward a specified responsibility. The second grade teacher should become the best possible second grade teacher. The high school English teacher should teach English in the most effective way possible. In most all instances, the people involved have accepted a full-time professional responsibility in their given area of concern.

   The community educator, especially in the early stages of Community Education development, is forced to work with part-time people. This group often perceives their part-time assistance as a means of making a few extra dollars – nothing more.

While it is difficult to change individuals involved on a full-time basis, it is even more difficult to obtain change if the involvement is perceived only as a chance to obtain some additional income.

3. Earlier in the chapter, the general problem of underfunded in-service efforts was discussed. While this is a general problem faced by all who attempt to provide in-service programs, it is even more acutely faced by the community educator. In the early stages of development, when in-service is most needed, finances are the most difficult to obtain. It is a simple fact of life that most Community Education programs are not adequately funded initially. The demand for existing dollars, then, is much greater in Community Education than it would be in programs that have had time to develop and establish at least a minimal financial base. Community educators often face the difficult dilemma of adequately supporting essential in-service efforts at the expense of establishing two or three essential community services.

4. Because Community Education does not limit education to the schools, or its in-service efforts to teachers or administrators, any in-service planned must deal with extremely diverse groups with specified unique functions within the general program effort. It is impossible to establish one or two major in-service efforts to adequately serve all groups. How, for example, could you combine the in-service needs of teachers in the program with those of the building directors; the needs of school administrators with those of paraprofessionals; or the needs of the school board with those of a staff employed to provide high school completion opportunities to adults.

Unique diverse needs require many different in-service efforts in Community Education. Directors must consider the scope of the program, the diversity of the groups involved, and the in-service requirements of each.

Who Needs In-Service and Why?

The preceding pages have described general in-service needs and the diverse groups with whom community educators must concern themselves.

Establishing an In-Service Program to Meet Staff Needs

Each of the groups has unique needs that must be met through different techniques.

The administration, for example, must have a fairly sophisticated understanding of the concept before true support can be gained. An in-service program for this group must be designed to clearly portray the concept and define the role the administrator will play within the concept. It must be done on an intellectual sophisticated level, incorporating a rationale for the concept based upon existing knowledge in the field.

Teachers also need to understand the concept and to identify their role within it. The specific concerns of this group, however, focus upon the classroom and the effect Community Education will have upon the relationship between students and themselves, parent involvement, and increased community expectations. In-service efforts for teachers must include methods of relieving teacher anxiety, of demonstrating the positive impact of community involvement, and stressing the importance of educational relevance to the needs of the community.

In addition to teachers and administrators, it is also important to include the school's noncertified staff in an in-service effort. If this group can develop an acceptance of the concept, they can then accept work schedule changes, new responsibilities, and new problems with less difficulty. In-service efforts for this group must stress the important role that noncertified personnel play in Community Education, attempting to make this group feel that they are an important part of the team.

Because of the broad nature of Community Education, in-service efforts can not be limited to the staff of the public school. In-service efforts must also be developed for social and governmental agencies, lay citizens, and the business and industrial community. Each of these groups, while unique, share the need to understand their role in Community Education, the advantages that may be obtained through their involvement, and the new sense of purpose that may be established in the entire community.

As previously indicated, extensive planning for in-service is crucial. Prior to involving others in the in-service planning process, it is important to clarify what is to be accomplished in your own mind. This often can best be established by utilizing outside professional assistance. A consultant with special expertise in in-service planning may be employed to assist. A director of one of the Regional Community Education Centers that exist around the country may be called upon. The services of these centers are provided by people with extensive experience and expertise. State and national Community Education associations exist that provide consultant services to community educators. In addition to this, extensive reading may also provide appropriate assistance.

SECTION V

Economic Considerations in Community Education

CHAPTER XI

Including the Economic Sector of the Community

It has been said that many foreign visitors studying the United States' economic system believe that the one prominent difference between our system and others is a universally well-educated work force. Education, it is believed, has been the major force behind the expansion and development of our economic system. These same observers point out that the people who ignore this observation most, and place the least emphasis on education as a necessary part of economic growth, are the Americans themselves—especially American businessmen and industrialists.

Americans have long cherished the value of education and have demonstrated support through the development of an educational system that is designed to educate every child in the nation through grade 12. No other nation has ever experimented with an educational program on such a broad scale and attempted to make education the right of every child. Our belief in education is unquestioned. Until recently, however, we have never attempted to study the relationship between our massive support for education and the phenomenal economic growth of our country to the greatest industrial nation in the world in less than 200 years.

Industrialists and economists are now beginning to recognize this relationship and attempt to determine the extent of inter-dependency between the economic system and education, and to determine the relationship between increasing educational levels in the country and increasing national income.

Several years ago one complete issue of the *Kaiser Aluminum News* was devoted to education. One of the sections in this issue entitled, "The Grand Investment," dealt specifically with the relationship between educational development and economic growth. The following quotation from this article is especially interesting because it is presented in a magazine produced by a major industrial corporation.

". . . . . . Up until the mid 1950's it was pretty generally believed that the way to increase national income was through reinvestment of capital in material things: factories, machinery, rolling stock, power generators, etc.. . . . The converse of this belief was that money invested in education was at the expense of capital investment and to that extent reduced the growth of national income. . . . . . .

Economists at the Massachusetts Institute of Technology began, about ten years ago, to examine the basic assumption that capital investment in material things was the primary source of the increase in the national income. . . . They discovered that changes in the size of the work force, together with changes in the volume of physical capital, accounted for only about 15 percent of the growth of production in the United States. This left a whopping 85 percent of the growth unexplained by traditional investment theory."[1]

The article continues with an attempt to explain the difference:

"Along about the same time, a parallel study was being conducted at the University of Chicago on the relationship between the level of education and household incomes, in which there appeared an invariable correspondence between higher education and higher income. When the two studies were put together, it was apparent that education and a rising national income were directly linked."[2]

---

[1] "The Grand Investment," *Kaiser Aluminum News,* Vol. 25, No. I, p. 27.

[2] Ibid. p. 27.

Including the Economic Sector of the Community

To further support the linkage between education and economic growth, Professor Charles S. Benson of the University of California – Berkely states:

> "Now, national income, that most central of all economic statistics, is the sum 'factor income,' and by far the most important of 'factor incomes' are wages and salaries (the others are rent, interest, dividends, etc.). When the work force of a country receives more education, the corresponding rise in their levels of wages and salaries is translated directly into increases in the national income . . . . . Current estimates indicate that between 20 and 40 percent of our growth is a result of expenditures on schooling."[3]

In another article entitled "The Economic Value of the Community School Concept to Local Business," Mr. Joseph Anderson, former general manager of A.C. Spark Plug Division of General Motors provides some similar insights. He believes that as people gain better and greater amounts of education their tastes change and are expanded and that there is then an increased desire for new, different, and better products. These increased desires will create a greater market for new homes, nicer furniture and decorations, and more appliances and conveniences. Mr. Anderson gives an excellent example of the result of ignoring the direct relationship between economic growth and education.

A few years ago, Atlanta, Georgia, had the lowest per capita spending for public schools of any major city in the United States. This low tax assessment resulted in lower costs of operation and the Chamber of Commerce of Atlanta used this as an enticement to new business to locate in Atlanta. In an attempt to change the thinking of the business community, the superintendent of the Atlanta Public Schools did some additional research and found that Atlanta had not only the lowest educational cost per child, but also the lowest annual spending per capita for retail goods. His research gave some validity to

---

3 Charles S. Benson, "The Rationale Behind Investment In Education," *Education Age,* March/April, 1967, p. 14.

his supposition that business was directly and adversely affected when good education was not considered a vital and necessary part of a total community's needs. [4]

Thus it appears that there is an interrelationship between economic growth and educational development. While research concerning this relationship is incomplete and no accurate ratios of education to economic growth can yet be ascribed, little doubt can exist that a direct and interdependent relationship does exist.

Accepting this conclusion, then, it would seem logical that the business and educational communities would mutually benefit from a close working relationship. Educators, through increased support, could provide greater and more diversified educational services; and the business and industrial community could not only expect greater long term economic growth, but could also take advantage of educational expertise in short-term training and retraining programs.

The basis for a good partnership exists. The vehicle for establishing that partnership also exists in the Community Education concept. The problem becomes that of getting the business community to recognize the obvious advantages available to them and to then establish dialogue between educators and businessmen to begin some joint undertakings.

Some Ideas for Action

To begin any partnership, potential partners must realize that a joint undertaking can be profitable and worthwhile. Community educators' needs for additional funding and business' needs for profit, economic growth, and community involvement and support, are some of these reasons. Finding appropriate ways to present these factors to businessmen and to gain acceptance of the concepts presented here can be quite difficult. This is especially true in light of prior relationships between educators and businessmen and an underlying distrust of each other's motivation.

---

[4] Joseph Anderson, "The Economic Value of the Community School Concept to Local Business," *The Community School and Its Administration,* Vol. VII, No. 9, May, 1969, p. 1.

Including the Economic Sector of the Community

To initiate positive contacts and positive relationships with the business community, care and planning should be given to how this can most effectively be done.

To start, a careful study of the large businesses and manufacturers in the area should be made. An informal attempt should be developed to determine the companies that are most aggressive and farsighted, that have previously demonstrated an interest in education, and that have previously demonstrated concern for community growth and development. This can be done by talking with knowledgeable people in the community about those businesses that have demonstrated concern in the past for the community and community development. By finding the companies that are concerned with community development, chances are greatly increased that they will be more receptive to any suggestion for a partnership between the schools and business. Once these companies have been identified, an attempt should be made to assess the top level executives within these companies and determine those which display the same interests and concerns. From the group of executives that seems most interested in community development and educational growth, individuals should be selected who might be most receptive to a closer working relationship with the educational community and who would not oppose the possibility of some financial support. Any or all these men, then, become the initial contact with the local business community.

This selection process, while informal, forces the community educator to analyze the business and industrial community and select individuals who probably will have some interest in Community Education and the change that is being attempted through the schools.

If these businessmen can be convinced of the value of joining business and educational forces, they can assist in obtaining the support of other community business leaders.

Once the business executives have been selected, planning for the first meeting should begin. A luncheon meeting is often advantageous because of the pleasant atmosphere created and because the busy executive is often most available at this time. The meeting should be fairly small and informal. It should include the executives who have been invited and anyone they might wish to bring with them, the superintendent and a board member, the community educator, and any additional people who might add to the meeting. The reasons for meeting and the desired outcome of the meeting should be pre-establsihed. There are normally three possible and realistic goals for an initial meeting of this nature:

1. To generally describe the proposed program and to promote an *awareness* of what is being attempted within the business community.

2. To describe an existing or planned Community Education program and to gain a commitment from the executives present for involvement of a much larger percentage of the local business community in a similar meeting at a later date.

3. To describe Community Education generally, or a special program within it, and to gain a financial commitment from the executives present in support of the program or specific parts of it.

Any of these goals are acceptable and the selection of any one of the three must be based upon local needs, urgency of community problems, and predetermined long or short-term goals. It is suggested, however, that number two offers the greatest promise in most cases. This option does not preclude financial assistance, but it does offer the opportunity for a greater involvement of the total business community and a potential for greater financial commitment from many companies, rather than the support of just a few. Further, assuming the selection process used in determining your initial contacts was adequate, there are strong possibilities that the individuals selected are considered leaders in the business community. If this is so, then their vocal support at the inception of a program is as valuable as any financial contribution they might make.

Whatever goal is established for the meeting, the initial presentation must be planned around this goal and designed so that the conclusion brings the group naturally to a positive response to the questions being considered – is it a good idea or isn't it? Should we involve some of the other businessmen in the community or shouldn't we? Should we fund this program or not?

The presentation should be short and concise. It should clearly present the ideas that you have, including your perception of the

Including the Economic Sector of the Community

problems that you hope to solve and reasons why you think the approach you are presenting will be effective in solving these problems. This presentation should be well-prepared and developed. It can result in an important possible source of revenue and support, and should be treated as such. Finally, one word of caution – be honest! Know the difference between what you can accomplish, and what you wish you could accomplish. Don't be afraid to admit that program limitations exist and that what you propose will not cure all of society's ills and problems.

Once initial contacts have been established and you begin working with the business community, it is essential that you constantly work toward maintaining their support. This can best be done through continued involvement and communication of what you are doing. Invitations to community banquets, adult graduations, special visitation programs, etc. can greatly assist in showing some of the positive results of the program. An occasional newsletter, personal note, or the mailing of a news item can greatly assist in maintaining interest and keeping your key businessmen informed.

It is also recommended that as business and industrial support grows and develops, a council of businessmen be established to assist the director in maintaining good two-way communications and to provide an opportunity to discuss new ideas and plans, new programs, or new attacks on old problems and continuing conerns.

Economic Value to the Community

No discussion of the economic value of education would be complete without including the major economic impact Community Education has upon program participants and the community at large.

Extensive statistics are available demonstrating the relationship between the level of educational achievement and annual income. Certainly a concept that provides programs that improve basic skills, and expand educational levels has a major economic impact. As individual vocational and educational skills increase, potential earning power also grows. Increased earnings mean increased spending, and people who might have been tax burdens become contributors.

The community as a whole, also reaps benefits. As a pride in ones community is developed, and as a feeling of concern for others grows, one logical result should be a reduction in vandalism and delinquency. Communities presently expend enormous sums to replace and repair facilities damaged through vandalism. Much of this money could be spent more positively if communities could develop a sense of oneness; a community esprit de corps.

The community could also benefit financially by avoiding costly duplication of services. As a community begins to work together, and agencies begin to cooperate with each other, former duplicated services can be eliminated and replaced by new services for the same financial expenditure.

CHAPTER XII

Financing Community Education

Probably the most frequent excuse for failure of communities to begin Community Education relates to financing. School districts, already hard pressed for operating and building funds, are reluctant to take on additional financial obligations when their source of funds for traditional programs are already diminishing.

One of the greatest errors one can make in advising school districts in this matter is to attempt to convince school boards that such a program will not cost them any additional money. It should be obvious that the addition of personnel and programs is bound to add increased costs to the school district. In addition, to attempt to start Community Education without financial commitment from the school district itself is to instigate the old "something for nothing" game, and the results are often disappointing. The problem of financing, therefore, frequently boils down to the following situation – how can a school district secure initial funds for the implementation of Community Education, and how can the same district become financially supportive of such a program in the same manner as they support their other educational endeavors?

Community Education Costs

To imply that Community Education will not add to the financial responsibilities of the school district is to doom Community Education from the beginning. The very essence of Community Education is one of opening buildings for more hours of the day and more days of the year, to expand the educational responsibilities of the school district and to provide community services which have not been previously offered by the schools. To do this will obviously require additional funds.

First, there will be an investment in personnel. While many school districts start Community Education with only one full-time administrator, it is hoped that ultimately there will be at least one director for every school building in the school district; and this might be minimal. The needs of the community may require some buildings to employ more than one person in order to carry out the varied functions of a full-fledged Community Education program. There may be a need for specialized personnel such as social workers, home counselors, etc., to work effectively with members of the community. In addition, there will be a need for secretarial assistance at each building level.

The program within the building will necessitate additional personnel costs also. There will be a need for instructors to handle the various classes which are offered. This cost will vary depending on the training required, supply and demand, and the teacher's master contract. Included in this cost will be salaries for persons who supervise activities. There will also be a cost factor for custodial help. Not only will there be additional cleaning, but many districts require a custodian to be present whenever any activity takes place in the school building. Other program costs include the additional heat and light required when such programs are going on in the buildings.

In addition to added personnel, there will be some other cost factors as well. One of these will be the cost of special equipment. When the areas of programming are expanded, extra equipment is required. For example, if a community room is established and set aside for the use of community residents, then there is a need for such things as a stove, sink, refrigerator, dishes, card tables, and other items necessary for equipping such a room properly. In certain communities, equipment such as washers, dryers, and sewing machines might be added. If special classes are offered to the community, then there will be an expenditure for appropriate sized tables, chairs, educational equipment, recreational equipment and vocational and avocational tools and machinery which may not currently be in the building. Other facilities may also have to be added or changed in order to carry out a Community Education program. For example, it may be necessary to provide expanded parking facilities, lighting for the parking area and playfields, outside drinking fountains and toilets, and a variety of facilities designed to serve adults as well as children.

Added to these will be administrative costs for such things as office space, telephones, supplies, travel and office equipment.

An enumeration of the preceding cost factors may at first seem overwhelming and could result in a reluctance to start a Community Education program. Closer scrutiny, however, will reveal that the problem is not as great as it might first appear. First of all, the costs listed include the total of those in a sophisticated program. Most programs start slowly and the encumbrance of cost will require additional monies, others will be assumed through better utilization of existing programs and facilities, reducing the anticipated total expenditure.

It is quite obvious, however, that the implementation of Community Education will require additional monies, and one of the first questions asked by boards of education will be, "Where will we get the money to start such a program?" Their concern is legitimate, particularly since they are being asked to expend funds in an area not usually judged appropriate for the spending of public school monies. There is therefore a need for information as to what sources of money are available for the implementation and development of Community Education.

Sources of Money

Federal Government

Many Community Education programs have found substantial amounts of funding available through various federal projects. No effort is made here to identify all of these sources since they are constantly changing. However, in the past many of the programs such as the Office of Economic Opportunity, the Elementary Secondary Act, the Open Spaces Act, the Higher Education Act and others have furnished funds by which programs have been started and continually supported. The key in getting such assistance has been to analyze such legislation for its applicability to Community Education and then submit a proposal for funding. In general, success for such funding has come from the ingenuity of the persons writing the proposal in adapting the legislation to their particular needs. Rather than be dissuaded by the title of legislation, they have attempted to work within the guidelines to get federal monies for their districts. An example of this is the Open Spaces Act. While interpreted by many as a device for assisting in the development of park areas for the city ghettos, some rural areas have successfully obtained funds to develop recreation areas within their own communities.

One caution should be noted in the use of federal funds for Community Education. Current federal assistance is aimed at programs for disadvantaged and urban school districts. While there is no question that community educators should consider the use of such funds where appropriate, they must be careful not to get so involved with such funding that their programs become identified as poverty-related and subsequently result in the implication that Community Education is only for the poor and disadvantaged. The director must also be certain that he does not become so involved in the development of programs which are federally funded that he loses sight of the total concept and therefore minimizes the potential effect of Community Education for his community.

State Government

The advice given for seeking federal monies might also be given for state funds. Most states have allocated funds for special programs designed to meet state educational priorities. With a little imagination, proposals can be written so that certain portions of the Community Education program can be funded from these sources.

Most applicants to the Community Education programs are those state funds appropriated for adult and vocational education. These

Financing Community Education

funds not only support the programs for which they are intended, but often provide excess funds. In the beginning, when Community Education is expected to pay its own way from external funding, it is important that the school board be convinced that all funds such as these be channeled into Community Education and not absorbed in the general fund. It is difficult enough to find sources of funding for Community Education without expecting such programs to be money-makers for the traditional programs.

In addition to adult and vocational educational funds, certain states have specific appropriations for Community Education programs. Some of these states have allocated funds on the basis of a head count participation in Community Education classes. For example, for each person enrolled in a Community Education class there is a flat fee paid to the district. Other states are financially aiding Community Education by including specific budgeted amounts in their state aid formula for Community Education. Financial arrangements for this type of aid range from reimbursing a portion of each community school director's salary to providing a grant to each building which has a building director. In each case, the dollars are to be spent on persons (salaries) rather than programs.

Probably the most important part of such financial assistance is that it provides the incentive for starting Community Education in the school district by supplying some of the necessary initial funds. It also tends to legitimatize Community Education by putting an official state stamp of approval on this concept as a bona fide part of the educational plan.

Business and Industry

No group stands to profit more from Community Education than local business and industry. Conversely, few people realize the commitment which this group has toward support of their local community. Almost every type of private enterprise expects to contribute funds to public endeavors as a part of their responsibility to that community. The fact is that few persons are really aware of the extent of the contribution business and industry might be willing to make. They tend to evaluate potential of giving on the basis of their own incomes and experiences. If there is ever a place where we must "think big" it is in regard to this type of giving. There are numerous examples across the country where school districts have obtained continued financial support from local business and industry in an amount which financially supported the bulk of their Community Education programs.

Philanthropy

There are many more sources of financing, both individual and foundation, than one might expect. Some of these sources are local persons who are looking for worthwhile projects to contribute to. Motivation for this, as in business and industry, is both personal satisfaction and tax considerations. Some persons wish to identify themselves with good causes by giving portions of their personal incomes to such activities. Other persons have been given tax-sheltered exemptions for the purpose of donating to worthy causes, and they are required by law to expend their funds on such enterprises.

In considering philanthropy, one should also look outside the community. There are numerous foundations in all parts of the country looking for promising practices with which to identify. Community Education has proved to be an attractive venture for many such foundations, and communities should not overlook this source of funding.

Local Service Clubs and Organizations

These groups, while often not as great a potential source as others, do have monies to assist Community Education. Although not able to provide extensive revenues individually, their combined efforts can be considerable. One approach in getting money from these sources is to have them finance a specific portion of the Community Education program. By taking on a limited project, such as providing roller skates, or other types of equipment, they can make a significant contribution. This technique for fund raising also provides a meaningful identity and involvement for the participating groups.

Other Governmental Agencies

This is often one of the most overlooked sources from which money is available. Many of the programs in Community Education, particularly as they relate to recreation and community service, will be concerns of other governmental units in the community, such as the county, township, and city. Often these units have allocated funds for activities and are either expending them in a somewhat haphazard, uncoordinated manner or are not using the allocations because the amount is not large enough to hire the needed personnel. By consolidating these funds and channeling them through a Community Education program, duplication will be eliminated, resulting in better programs and increased activities.

Social Agencies

In most communities there are already many programs being carried on by social agencies with an extensive expenditure of funds. The problem here is again one of coordination. By drawing upon the resources of these agencies, and assuring a coordination of their activities with those of other community agencies, many programs and services can be offered without additional expenditures.

When activities are coordinated and duplication eliminated, money that is saved can be utilized to provide new services to the community that could not previously be provided.

Fund Raising

This source of funding offers a greater potential than might be expected. At first, one tends to think of this activity in terms of such things as pancake suppers, bake sales and the like. Such activities generally are limited in their fund raising ability and can contribute only a limited number of dollars. It should be kept in mind, however, that for the purposes of Community Education, this type of activity offers two things: First, it does raise some money, if only in limited amounts. Of more importance, however, is the fact that in such a joint effort, members of the community get involved in a worthwhile activity which brings them closer together, engendering a spirit of community. This fact alone, may be ample reason for engaging in such an activity.

Community Education: From Program to Process

Fund raising also may have a greater potential for raising dollars than we realize. Many school fairs, for example, raise thousands of dollars. Some communities have raised money on such things as raffles in which the prizes are of considerable worth. Income from this type of activity is often in the thousands of dollars and the profit can be even higher, if the prizes are donated or purchased at cost. One community has an annual auction in which items contributed by wealthy persons in the community are auctioned off to these same people. The charitable mood of the bidders results in a considerable income for the Community Education program.

In general, the techniques for raising money in this fashion are limited only by the imagination of those involved. One of the prime motivating factors is that people will often make a greater effort when the cause is known beforehand and when it is a cause in which they believe. So often, fund raising activities in education raise the money first and decide on how it shall be spent later. By having Community Education or a specific project within it as the intended recipient, it is frequently possible to achieve greater input and provide greater satisfaction to members of the community.

Class Fees

Payment for the programs by participants in the program is often a good source of funding. Participants in most activities should be expected to pay either an established fee or a pro-rated fee for those courses which they wish to take. In general, most people are able and willing to accommodate such tuition. Provisions should be made to provide free tuition to those who cannot financially afford to enroll in courses which they need or would like to take. Some programs also provide for a variable fee structure so that those who can afford to pay more can provide surplus monies which can be used in courses where the participants are less able to afford the total cost of their class. Thus, people enrolled in a class in bridge may pay enough to cover the cost of their class plus a portion of the class in nutrition established for welfare mothers.

Local Taxes

The ultimate goal for financing Community Education should be to obtain funds from the same sources from which we fund our existing educational programs. If one truly believes in Community Education, then he believes that it is an expanded and legitimate part of the total education structure. As such, it should receive the same financial support as existing programs. To attempt to make Community Education pay its own way, is merely a stopgap technique, acceptable only as a temporary situation. As long as school districts insist that Community Education directors must find their own funding, they will continue to have programs which achieve less than the total potential of Community Education.

This means, then, that Community Education should be financed from the same tax structure as that provided for traditional education. In fact, many districts discover that as they make education more relevant and meet the educational needs of more people in their communities, taxpayers are willing to approve the money needed for such programs. Once Community Education has had an opportunity to develop in a community, categorical millage for Community Education is often the easiest millage on which to get favorable voter reaction.

In-Kind Services

In evaluating program costs, we must look at another source of funding which is not given in dollars, but which has the same effect on the financial needs of Community Education. This is probably best described as in-kind services. These services fall into several categories but have one common denominator. They all include characteristics which result in a donation of time or materials which if not provided would result in extra costs and would require additional dollars to provide. These in-kind services then are volunteered time, materials or techniques offered to Community Education which stand in lieu of money and thus serve to supplant some of the financial needs of Community Education.

Free or Inexpensive Programs

There are many fine programs which are either free or very inexpensive and which are available to the school district if solicited. Such programs as first-aid courses by the Red Cross, gun safety by law enforcement agencies, retirement planning by social security offices, and boat safety by the sheriff's department are usually available at no cost in most communities. In addition, many clubs and organizations such as kennel clubs and riding associations offer free courses in their area of specialty. Social agencies, too, have various courses for the public and are anxious to find facilities in which to present them. Business and industry are also good program sources. Add to this the many other educational and information programs available which are one or two sessions in length, and communities will find a variety of offerings available at little or no cost.

Another point to keep in mind is that many good programs have little or no expense. The cost, for example, of opening the gym to the men in the community for recreational purposes is minimal. Similarly, the opening of a classroom or a cafeteria for the purpose of card playing or bingo by a group of senior citizens can be done at a cost which is negligible. If prizes are necessary, the participants can furnish them themselves in the form of "white elephants," inexpensive gifts, or canned goods. In a like manner, many other activities can be carried on which provide for the needs of the community and yet are cost-free.

Voluntary Help

Some of the personnel needs can be met by using volunteers from the community. Each community has people who have special skills or hobbies and who are willing to donate their time. Some persons will want to volunteer because they want to be useful, while others will be motivated to work for little or nothing because of their tax status in relation to their retirement income. In some cases, these persons will have the background to teach special classes or offer unique programs. Others will prove useful as supervisors or aides or in assisting with certain custodial duties. It should be kept in mind that while these services will reduce the expenses of the program, the fact that the individual is garnering some personal rewards from his endeavor is equally important and should suffice to justify the use of such persons.

Donated Items

The donation of many needed programming items is also of financial value. Such things as cards, horseshoes, tables, games, and any type of equipment or materials which will enhance the programs are valuable. It may also be possible to obtain items from local businesses which are given as a goodwill gesture.

Paraprofessionals Employment Opportunities

There are many occasions when local persons are capable of doing the job expected in a given area without having all the skills of a professional in that area. For example, some types of supervision or secretarial work can be done effectively by these members of the community. By employing such persons at reduced salaries, considerable savings are realized.

Reassignment of Personnel

Since personnel costs are frequently the greatest cost factor in Community Education, this is the area in which the greatest savings can be made. One technique for doing this is through the reassignment of current personnel. Some teachers, for example, can be given different schedules so that their services can be better utilized to cover both the regular day program, and additional activities that may occur at other times.

If we can view the regular school day as not being sacred in terms of teacher assignments, then certain teachers, such as art or music teachers, might be assigned to start their day earlier or later so that their special talents might be available to students or adults either before or after the regular school day.

In a like manner, custodial help might be more beneficially assigned. In many instances, the bulk of the custodial staff is on duty when they are least needed. The school day frequently allows for limited custodial activity, but this is often the time when most of the custodians are available. The result is that often either a limited amount of janitorial service is carried out or else the school activities are limited or disturbed by such things as window washing, sweeping, or lawn mowing. Having a minimal force in the daytime with the reassignment of other staff members to late afternoon or late evening schedules makes more sense since custodians can work without conflict with students and teachers. By readjusting this schedule to one in which the cleaning is performed by a night crew, it is possible to maintain the building at the same level with little or no additional staff.

One additional personnel saver is recommended with extreme limitations. It is possible, in the beginning stages of the program, to have a part-time community school director. This can be accomplished by employing a building director who teaches half-days, and works half-days as a director. This may be an acceptable way of getting into Community Education as long as it is done with the full understanding that it is a temporary arrangement. Such an assignment will result in a very limited operation which is primarily program-oriented. However, if the intent is to initiate Community Education gradually and show the value of such a program when no other avenue is open, then such a technique may prove beneficial.

The means of financially supporting a Community Education program need not be limited to those presented here. With the right person as director, funding is frequently not as big a problem as often anticipated, and the ingenuity and inventiveness of such a director will often uncover many unique ways of overcoming financial needs. It would be a serious error, however, to fail to re-emphasize a point made earlier about funding in relation to the board of education. The philosophy of Community Education is an expansion of the traditional school philosophy. It is based on the belief that the educational needs of all communities are larger than those served by the traditional programs. It implies that schools should take on larger responsibilities in identifying and helping to solve community problems. It is a legitimate function of the school and as such it is entitled to the same financial considerations as other school programs. Eventually, then, Community Education should be supported in the same fashion as the traditional school program, and once a school board commits itself to Community Education, it has the moral responsibility of providing the financial means necessary to support a sound Community Education program.

CHAPTER XIII

Establishing a Budget

"The tail that wags the dog" is an expression often used to describe the budgeting process in the public schools. All too often the expression is appropriate in educational budgeting, and available dollars do determine educational programming. Although financial limitations certainly cannot be ignored, proper budgeting procedure can be used to advantages and can assist in the planning of the very best educational program possible within specified fund limitations. Further, proper budgeting can demonstrate the extent of need for additional funding by indicating programs that should be attempted, but that must be eliminated or remain untried because of inadequate funding.

A budgeting process that is based upon the principles of sound programmed budgeting is of immeasurable assistance to the community educator because many people (including other educators) do not understand what Community Education is, what existing funds are used for and what services and opportunities are provided through these funds, as well as what expanded opportunities would be available through Community Education if additional funds were allocated. Program budgeting forces a community educator to think through his priorities and ultimately place program emphasis on what he considers most important.

Program or Performance Budgeting

The concept of program budgeting or performance budgeting has been discussed and encouraged in education for years. Recently, the basic concept has been expanded and refined and given a different title – Program Planning and Budgeting System (PPBS). This approach while utilizing new technology and sophisticated systems, is still an out-growth of the basic performance budgeting concept that educators have long considered.

There are four basic steps in establishing a good performance budget, each of which is essential to the final outcome.

1. Establishing program objectives on a priority basis.
2. Determining program activities necessary to reach the pre-established objectives.
3. Estimating expenditures required to support the pre-established programs.
4. Establishing evaluation criteria to determine the success or failure of the program. (This should be done in terms of long and short-range indicators.)

Once these four criteria have been fulfilled, the system becomes cyclical, in that the establishment of new objectives and programming depends upon the evaluation process and the feedback built into the budgeting system.

Let us now turn to a step-by-step approach to establishing a performance budget.

Development of Program Objectives

Step 1

An important part of any Community Education program is the determination of community needs and the establishment of a program to meet those needs. Community problems, by their very nature, are often complicated, vague, and difficult to define. Programs designed to solve these problems are difficult, if not impossible, to evaluate if no clear objectives are defined in terms of desirable program outcome as it relates to problems the program is designed to solve.

It is important at this point to recognize the difference between the establishment of goals and the establishment of objectives. Goals can be, and often are, very general statements of desirable end results with little or no specificity. They often are impossible to measure. Objectives state the problem in very specific measurable terms and break the desired goals into their various cognitive, affective and psychomotor variables. Specific objectives of this type are referred to as behavioral objectives.

Example: As a community educator, you have determined that one of the major problems faced by your community is a rather high illiteracy rate. This illiteracy rate has contributed to many problems within the community: a high unemployment rate; a large population segment that does not exercise its political rights or accept its political obligations; a group of people with very negative and somewhat hostile attitudes toward the school and society; and a segment of the population whose negative attitude toward education creates within their children equally negative feelings toward the educational process.

The general *goal,* then, is to provide expanded basic literacy skills to the adult segment of the population requiring increased reading, writing and computational skills and to improve their attitudes toward the society.

It is easy to see that this goal certainly would be difficult to measure and it certainly does not cover all of the problems posed.

The establishment of behavioral objectives assists in clarifying specific purposes and when these behavioral objectives are properly developed, they can be measured at a later specified date to determine success or failure, or the degree of success.

Within the goal of "providing basic literacy skills to the adult segment of our population requiring increased reading, writing, and computational skills and to improve their attitudes toward society," there are several variables that must be considered:

1. Is attitude change concerning education and society an objective?

2. Is it desirable or possible to change the attitudes of the children of illiterate adults through the improvement of the parent's attitudes?

3. Should the program be designed to improve participation within the political framework?

4. How many people can be served within the population segment described?

5. Will increased literacy skills increase employment opportunities or job promotion opportunities?

6. How extensive should the literacy program be and what could be considered success or failure?

Each of the preceding questions was developed from some of the rationale that established the basic goal, even though the goal did not include this many variables.

Assuming that each of the first five questions is answered positively, it is then necessary to establish *behavioral objectives* within the established goal. Six questions have been stated and must be redefined in objective measurable terms. Some possible ways of approaching this are:

1. Participants enrolled in a basic literacy program will improve their attitudes toward education and become more receptive to education. This improved attitude will be assessed subjectively by the instructor at the end of one academic year and in objective terms by reviewing the participant's absence and tardiness record to determine if any improvement has occurred between the time the participant entered the program and the end of the academic year. Whether the participant plans to continue in the program another year will be another criteria used to determine success in improving participant attitudes.

2. The children of the participants enrolled in the basic literacy program should significantly improve in their own educational program within the public schools. This improvement should be evidenced in the first year by improved attendance and reduced tardiness, and within three years by a general improvement in grades.

3. The participants in the basic literacy program should gain a greater appreciation for the political process within a democratic system and a greater acceptance of responsibility within the system. This shall be determined by reviewing participant's registration and voting records preceding enrollment in the program and then reviewing these same criteria after one academic year. Increased registration and voting should be evidenced by the group. Pre- and post-examinations shall also be made regarding participants' affiliation with civic and charitable organizations. Increased involvement should be evidenced by the group at the end of one academic year.

4. The program will be considered a success in terms of enrollment if five percent (x number of students) of the total target population is enrolled within the first month of program operation. Upon completion of five years, the program will be considered a success if it has enrolled 20 percent (x number of students) of the total target population, and these students have averaged one year of participation in the program.

5. Participants enrolled in the basic literacy program should gain expanded employment opportunities as a result of new skills and attitudes. This will be measured through a questionnaire administered to all adults who started with the program at the end of two years. The questionnaire will specifically ask:

    A. Have you been employed in a new position during the last two years?

    B. Were you previously unemployed?

    C. Do you feel your employment was the result of this program?

D. Have you received a job promotion within the last two years?

E. Do you feel this promotion was the result of this program?

6. Participants enrolled in the basic literacy skills will improve their reading, writing, and computational skills by a minimum of one grade level at the completion of the first academic year and improve as a group an average of 1.5 grade levels. This improvement shall be determined by a pre- and post-test utilizing the XXX XXX Basic Skills Inventory.

It is important to note that while many of the behavorial objectives are unsophisticated, they are an attempt to evaluate the varied objectives of the general program goal and they do include some evaluation criteria for the affective program objectives; those objectives that are often avoided because of the difficulties they present in evaluation.

Step 2 — Planning a Program

Once behavioral objectives have been developed for each goal, established programs must be designed to meet the objectives specified. Program planning can no longer be the implantation of existing programs from other communities. Because program objectives have been established unique to the community, the program developed to meet these objectives must also be unique. The program planning process must be one of innovative thinking, cooperation with other educators and community leaders, and a willingness to experiment and develop new techniques. The programs that develop will probably be combinations of parts of existing programs that have been proven, unique variations of programs used for other purposes, and totally new and untried ideas. Because the programs developed will be unique and somewhat experimental, the evaluation criteria included in the behavioral objectives becomes increasingly important. The evaluation allows a determination of what has and has not worked and what should be changed to improve the program's effectiveness.

EXAMPLE: In the previous example, specific behavioral objectives were established; one of these objectives stated: "The program will be considered a success in terms of enrollment if five percent (x number of students) of the total target population is enrolled within the first month of program operation. Upon completion of five years, the program will be considered a success if it has enrolled 20 percent (x number of students) of the total target population, and these students have averaged one year of participation in the program."

It is evident that to meet this behavioral objective, a recruitment phase must be initiated as part of the planned program. To meet this objective, it will be necessary to consider questions such as:

1. How can I best communicate with the illiterate segment of the community?

2. What program aspects would most appeal to this group?

3. Which community agencies could assist in identifying the target population?

The basic point is that once you have established a behavioral objective, you must then determine the best means of meeting it. This process must be incorporated into the planning process for each behavioral objective. In the previous example, then, specific techniques and activities must be incorporated into the adult basic education program for each behavioral objective listed.

Step 3 – Estimation of Expenditures

Once the program plan has been established, it is necessary to put dollar amounts next to specific program parts. The sum total of all segments of each program and all programs designed to meet the goals and objectives of the community, plus the additional administrative and central office expenses assumed by the total Community Education program, becomes the dollar amount necessary to accomplish the stated objectives. It is at this point that revenues are compared to projected expenditures and decisions have to be made to reduce the proposed program to existing sources of revenue. This step, while painful in terms of what Community Education can and should do to improve the community, is relatively easy in terms of which program has to be cut. The importance of establishing program priorities was discussed previously. Assuming that these priorities have been established, the process of eliminating programs to meet specified budget limitations is simply the elimination of those programs lowest on the priority list. This step is extremely difficult since it eliminates many important activities and programs. The process described does, however, fulfill the promise made at the beginning of this chapter .... "proper budgeting procedure can be used to advantage and assist in planning the very best educational program possible within specified fund limitations ... and can demonstrate the extent of need for additional funding ...."

It is recommended that three separate budgets be developed:

1. A priority budget based upon existing revenues.

2. A budget including all possible revenues, even those that have not been assured, but which are possibilities.

3. A budget based upon the activities considered important, showing all programs and activities that were deemed necessary to meet the previously established goals and objectives.

The utilization of this budgeting process and the development of three distinct budgets has several advantages:

1. The community educator is forced to place priorities on everything that is attempted or recommended. He is forced to choose which specific programs are most important out of all things possible within the general framework of Community Education.

2. The community educator is forced to think beyond funds presently available and to look for new revenue sources. Once possible additional sources are considered and placed within the context of possible programming, the director is more willing to actively campaign for these funds. Further, since he knows exactly what he wants and why, he has a better chance of getting the money being sought.

3. Administrators within the school system become aware that the Community Education director is thinking ahead; that there are many additional benefits that could accrue to the community through him should additional funds be made available. This understanding is the genesis for later support when the administrative staff is determining the fund allocation for the school

system. Further, administrators observing a program operating on a priority basis without unlimited funds, are more receptive to the program, since their own programs within the system also suffer from underfunding.

Step 4 – Evaluating the Program and Priorities

This final step is one that takes place at times prescribed in the initial evaluation criteria. While it is not a part of the initial budgeting process, it is crucial to all future budgeting plans. Evaluation, based upon previously determined objectives, allows the Community Education director an opportunity to objectively evaluate what has been done and from this to re-evaluate his expenditures, his program priorities, and specific aspects of a given program to determine improvements that are necessary. This evaluation process is discussed extensively in Chapter 15 and therefore will not be dealt with in depth at this point.

Summary of Performance Budgeting

The past several pages have described a budgeting process that combines planning, programming, budgeting, and evaluating into one operation. This is quite unlike former budgeting practices that dealt only with dollars and cents and left the planning aspect to someone else. Good performance budgeting is really good curriculum planning, or a good evaluation system, or just good administration.

Once the budgeting process is completed, a format should be established to present the program ideas to others. William Roe in *School Business Management* describes a 13-step budget presentation that any budget presentation should include:

1. Title

2. Letter of Transmittal to the Board of Education

3. Table of Contents

4. Educational Philosophy and Objectives

5. A Look at the Years Ahead – Growing Pains

6. Educational Plan for Next Year

7. Financial Statement for Next Year — Summary of Expenditures and Receipts

8. Detailed Breakdown of Expenditures by Classification and Subclassification

9. Supporting Data for Expenditures

10. Comparison with Revenue and Expenditures for Previous Years

11. Comparative Data of Interest

12. A Discussion of Revenues

13. Conclusions" [1]

Establishing a System of Accounting

Once the budget has been established, a good accounting system will assure knowledge of exactly where you are at any time in relation to the established budget and will assure spending according to the plan that has been established.

To do this, an accrual system of accounting is recommended. This system assures an accurate determination of available funds at any given time because money is considered spent as soon as the actual liability for a given expenditure is incurred. For example, once some supplies are ordered, a certain amount of the supply budget is encumbered, even though money is not actually expended at that point. An accrual system shows these encumbrances and therefore allows one to avoid false estimates of available funds.

Each line item listed in the budget should be given an account number. To avoid confusion, the account number should be based upon

---

[1] William Roe, *School Business Management,* McGraw-Hill Book Company, Inc., New York, 1961, pp. 87-88.

Establishing a Budget

existing account numbers used in the school districts accounting system. Most school districts utilize a centralized accounting system and many directors feel it unnecessary to maintain their own records. It is recommended here that directors of Community Education maintain their own books to assure knowing exactly how much money is available at any one time and to assure a check on the total budget expenditures that they are responsible for.

An accrual system similar to the following example should be developed: (See page 226)

You will notice that the unencumbered balance is a total of $695.00, even though the items listed under encumbrances have not necessarily been paid. Under a cash accounting system a much larger balance would show. This could be misleading because a commitment has been made to pay the encumbered items, even though they have not yet been paid.

As the year progresses and funds that had been encumbered are actually expended, the amount expended is removed from the encumbrance account and listed as an actual expenditure. This does not change the amount listed in the unencumbered balance.

Establishing a good accounting system, like a good evaluation program, allows you to know where you are at any given point in time. A good evaluation program allows you to evaluate your progress toward stated objectives. A good accounting system allows you to evaluate your progress within a predetermined spending plan.

STUDENT ENRICHMENT

Account Number – 400

Total Appropriation – $5,000.00

Budget Line Item	Funds Appropriated	Cash Expended	Encumbrances	Unencumbered Balance
Reading for Fun 401	$ 500.00	Reading Material $100	Teacher Sal. $300 Supplies Ord. $100	$ 00.00
Teen Club 402	$ 700.00	Record Player $200 Volley Ball Set $50	Rec. Leader Sal. $300 Stud. Help. $100	$ 50.00
Science Club 403	$ 700.00	Microscope $250	Teacher Sal. $300 Science Kits Ord. $150	$ 00.00
Girl's Service Club 404	$ 500.00		Teacher Salary $300	$200.00
Boy's Intramural Football 405	$1,300.00	Uniforms $700	Rec. Leaders Sal. $250 Footballs $45	$305.00
Girl's Field Hockey 406	$ 700.00	Equipment $400	Rec. Leader Salary $250	$ 50.00
Conservation Club 407	$ 500.00	Field Trip $100	Teacher Salary $300	$100.00

SECTION VI

Planning for Facility Improvement, Evaluation and the Future

CHAPTER XIV

School Plant Planning

The proper design of any facility is dependent upon the use for which that facility is intended. Any other premise will result in an edifice which will prove to be disappointing to those who are to benefit from it and dysfunctional to those who are to use it.

The design of a school building is equally dependent upon identifying the objectives to be accomplished and the means by which these objectives are to be promoted. This has always been a truism in the design of educational facilities. When schools were to serve as town hall meeting sites, facilities were planned for such usage. When free transportation was not viewed as a public school function, schools were located on main highways for easy access.

In later years, school buildings became more sophisticated with the employment of architects whose main function was to design the school and oversee its construction. Unfortunately, there were many communities that acknowledged an expertise among architects and consequently often entrusted them with total responsibility for the entire building project. There was an assumption that if an architect knew the amount of money available and the type of buildings needs (elementary, junior high, or senior high) he could then proceed to develop an appropriate building on the basis of his know-how and experience.

Community Education: From Program to Process

Unfortunately, and to the chagrin of many districts, it was often discovered that the completed facility was not as they had expected and that many of the buildings lacked some of the basic ingredients of a good educational program. It soon became evident that in addition to the expertise of the architect, there was a need to have some input from the profession — namely, the teachers and administration. As a result, more and more school plant planners began to recommend that in addition to the architectural specifications relating to heat, lights, acoustics and physical space, there was a need to have educational specifications. These specifications were intended to provide the architect with vital information which only a teacher or experienced educator might possess. Through teacher involvement in planning, buildings were improved. The observations and suggestions related to such things as recessed drinking fountains, blackboard glare, lighting problems, coat space, boot and mitten storage, and placement of electrical outlets proved essential. By itemizing the things in a given building which had led to less effective learning, the architect was able to eliminate some of the previous problems in school buildings. Furthermore, by knowing the goals and objectives the teachers had established for their courses as well as the type of curricula to be offered and the techniques to be used, the architect was more realistically able to perform his function.

In most cases, other specifications were also added. By including the custodians, the secretaries, the bus drivers, the cafeteria workers, and others who were expected to function in this facility, it was possible to do a better all-around job, and the final product more nearly met the expectations of the staff members of that school.

To develop a community school requires a similar approach. The main difference being one of goals and involvement. While it is true that community members have been included in drawing school specifications, their task has generally been one of expressing their point of view as related to the traditional school program as perceived by parents.

To more clearly state the difference, we must first look at the goals and objectives of such a facility. In the book-centered era, the specifications were designed to match the goals of such an endeavor. If book-learning is the major theme, then it would logically follow that specifications would describe a building which concentrated on the role of a school which disseminates information, stresses academic discipline, and provides for the teacher-learner process of education.

In the child-centered era, which is the prevailing ideology today, the specifications required a different approach. Now it became necessary to provide for individualized instruction, with small group activity and facilities such as blackboards and bulletin boards scaled down to student size. With the focus on the learner, furniture became moveable, rather than stationary. Flexibility became the byword with chairs that adjusted, walls that moved, variance in space sizes and floors which could be walked or sat upon. Schools became the center of child or youth activity in which the very design suggested the exclusion of all others.

If one were then to attempt to identify the main difference in building design as suggested by Community Education, it would be necessary to identify the differences in goals and objectives. At the risk of educational heresy, Community Education believes that education facilities should be available to all persons with educational needs on an equal basis. Based upon this belief, it then becomes necessary to develop educational specifications which take into account the differences in age, size and availability of those to be served. Thus, if instead of serving a group of children from age 5 to 13, the school is to provide for the educational needs of all persons, then a different design is needed for that facility.

The job is not as formidable as it might seem. First of all, it is a matter of making an already flexible program more flexible. Secondly, it is a matter of involving the parents and others in planning the specifications. And, third, it is simply keeping in mind that students function quite well in the adult world at home and in their communities and can, in a similar fashion, function effectively in a learning climate designed for both adult and student use.

The first task, then, in developing Community Education specifications is to identify the goals and objectives for such a concept. While the overriding philosophy of Community Education will be the same for every community, it will be necessary to interpret this philosophy into behavioral objectives according to the specific needs of that community. To do this, it will be necessary to assess the community in order to understand the nature of the community and the areas of need. It will be necessary to have information about the physical factors of the community, the economic and business activity, social and governmental aspects, social agency operation, and other facilities available for Community Education. With this knowledge, and with community involvement, it now becomes possible to develop objectives and then begin to draw up educational specifications. Such specifications can then be used by the architect to design a school facility which will meet the needs of all it is to serve.

The culmination of these efforts will result in the construction of the building. The ensuing operation of the building will provide for programs and operation of activities within the building which, when

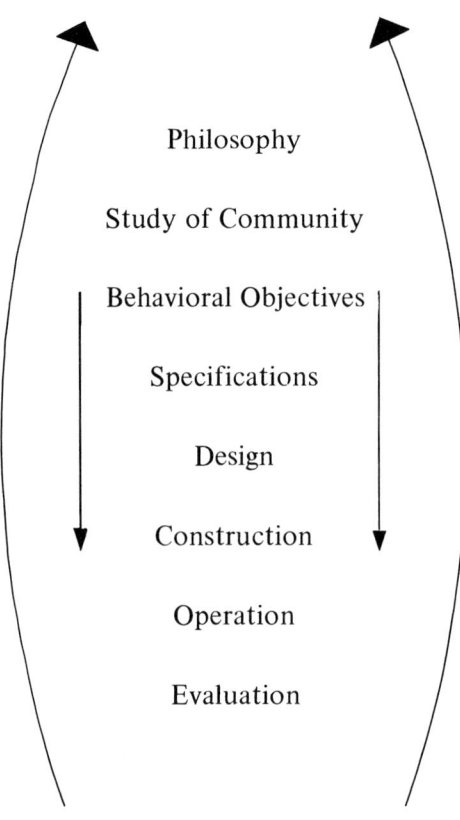

properly evaluated, will reflect back on how well the original philosophy has been interpreted and implemented. Evaluation then becomes the technique which allows the community to again look at its philosophy and regenerate the cycle so that such educational planning becomes an ongoing and self-perpetuating process.

The difference between this approach to school construction and previous methods is that frequently our past efforts have started at the specification level and the inputs have been primarily from a limited representation of those to be affected by the outcome.

It has already been strongly pointed out that since the design of the building will reflect community needs and objectives, each building program will be somewhat unique. Nevertheless, there has been a degree of commonality in districts which have designed buildings for Community Education. In order to assist districts in doing such planning, some specific suggestions follow for consideration.

Existing Facilities

In evaluating building needs for providing Community Education, one should consider existing facilities and avoid duplication when possible. There are many public and private facilities which frequently can provide adequate space and which are not receiving maximum usage. For example, there are existing school buildings, both public and private, which have special facilities such as shops, home economics facilities, and auditoriums which are both accessable and available. Such facilities should not be duplicated unless there is a definite need in order to provide for Community Education. In a similar manner, lodge halls, churches, government buildings, YMCA and YWCA facilities, theatres, public parks, recreation areas, facilities of business and industry, and even private homes provide suitable space where Community Education activities can take place. A part of facility planning is to make effective use of existing facilities through identification and coordination. Expensive duplication is an unacceptable and potentially dangerous approach in facility planning.

The School Site

There are some generally accepted guidelines for a traditional school site. School plant planners often give such figures as ten acres

Community Education: From Program to Process

plus one acre for each 100 students in an elementary school and 30 to 40 acres plus one acre for each 100 students for secondary schools. In designing a school for community use, these may not be adequate sizes. Added school usage and additional activities may necessitate more space. As the needs are identified, adjustments may be necessary in order to do an adequate job. The main caution here is that it is first necessary to identify the activities to be carried out before arriving at a site size. Accepting a suggested size, based on a traditional program, will result in inadequate space for carrying out the program.

School-Park Site

In many large cities, sites of the recommended size are simply not available. If they are available, the land expense is too great. In most large cities the cost of an acre of land would exceed one million dollars and building on an adequate site is prohibitive. In those areas, the need for Community Education and a community center, however, may be greater than in any other kind of community. To accomplish the objectives of Community Education, therefore, it becomes necessary to be more inventive and innovative. A high rise building with additional facilities below ground may provide part of the answer, and development of roof space and other available space may be the only means of increasing the facilities in the school.

One promising practice has been the school-park site. In most communities, planners have provided for city parks which are generally located throughout the city. Such parks are usually the only open space areas in the community and generally include such things as ball fields, picnic areas, play areas, playground apparatus and may even have a stream, lake, or pond. These parks make ideal playgrounds and are frequently least used at the time when school is in session.

With cooperative effort, it is possible to build a school building adjacent to such a site in a manner which gets the best possible usage from both facilities. The schools with buildings built to community specifications, can utilize the park area for their student activities. In fact, the park area is frequently better developed than a traditional school site and subsequently can provide for more and better student activities.

School Plant Planning

In a similar fashion, the school building can also serve the members of the community by adding to the facilities already present in the park. Community members now have meeting rooms, classrooms, a gym and other educational facilities. Furthermore, cooperative planning can result in joint financing of such facilities as a year-round attached swimming pool and a social service wing of the school, which can provide such things as an employment office, medical center, dental chair, counseling offices and other necessary community agencies. The end result is a combined venture which enhances the program for both the children and the community and, because of mutual planning, eliminates unnecessary duplication. This saves funds for the community which can then be used in better ways.

Outside Facilities

Consideration of the areas surrounding the school can frequently proceed from the assumption that such areas will include all the traditional facilities plus those needed to serve the additional activities of persons not currently provided for in such planning. Ball fields, play areas, hard surfaced sites, play apparatus, basketball facilities, underground wiring, proper drainage and nature trails are all things to be considered in such site development. In addition, however, the extended use of the site and the additional groups to be served will necessitate other considerations. Lighting of the activity areas will allow for evening activities. Increased parking will become necessary in order to accommodate adults who will want to use the facilities. Other types of games for more sedentary persons, such as horseshoe pits, and shuffleboard should be available. Pools for expanding summer programs should be considered, either as permanent facilities or by using some of the temporary or portable units which are available. Outside functions will demand toilets which should be constructed for winter as well as summer use. Hard surfaced areas for such things as roller skating should be provided and such areas can be constructed so that ice skating is available during the winter months. Picnic sites which can accommodate both family and group outings should also be included.

While such suggestions are certainly optimal and may not be possible in all communities, the limitation on such planning should be in terms of space and finances and not planning. Again, it is important to remember that the qualification for such planning is community need and interest and that these community interests and criteria should determine what things are planned for on the school site.

The Building

The primary consideration in planning the building is, again, to remember who is to use it and for what purposes it is to be used. Naturally, one of the prime considerations will be planning for the traditional student population which will be using the building. Everything should be done to develop a building which allows for maximum learning opportunity for the children who will attend school. The only restriction is that no design should be permitted which will eliminate other groups to be served by that facility.

The inputs for the traditional student program will not be discussed here. Suffice it to say that in addition to the needs of the students, a community-planned building should include the following things:

First, rooms should be planned so that in addition to those needed in the regular day program, there is enough space for room usage by other groups in the daytime. The usual procedure is to plan a building, such as an elementary school, for enough space to handle those students generated by the kindergarten sessions. Thus, for every kindergarten room (which can accommodate two classes a day) there would be two classes for each grade. It is simply recommended here that additional classrooms be provided for community use in the daytime.

There should also be a community room provided. This room should provide a comfortable space where citizens can meet, study, work or just relax. It should provide the kind of pleasant atmosphere necessary for attracting citizens to the school. The room should be ample enough to provide for at least 25 people. It should have a private access so that classes are not disturbed and citizens can feel a bit of privacy in using the space. The room should have comfortable furniture with chairs and tables available when needed. It should have a stove, refrigerator, sink and running water, cupboard space, dishes, curtains or drapes, carpeting, rest rooms, television, radio and may even have a washer, dryer and sewing machine. The room should be reserved for community use and requests by teachers or other school groups should not usurp the community's use of this room.

There should be a multi-purpose room or a gymnasium and an auditorium. Where cost permits separate facilities, it is best to have both. In many cases, however, and particularly in reference to elementary schools, the two facilities will have to be joined as one unit.

In the case of the separate theatre or auditorium, the main thing to keep in mind is that the facility is to be used for adult activities, plays, speeches, public forums, as well as student activities. Care should then be taken to assure that lighting, curtains, dressing rooms, seating, and other aspects of the design are in keeping with these extended activities.

In the gymnasium, the extra considerations are based on a similar logic. The ceiling, baskets, and other parts of the facility should be designed to accommodate the adults as well as children. There should be lockers, showers, and seating space for activities. The floor should be designed for the multiple activities which will take place there – gym, recreation league, roller skating, dances, etc. A portable stage can also increase the potential use of the gym.

There are still some other factors to be suggested in the design of a Community Education building. Zoning of the building for heat and lighting will make it easier to use parts of the building without having to heat and light the entire facility. In a similar way, zoning of the building by moveable gates will also help control the use of the building and limit occupancy to one area without opening the entire building when not necessary. Portable coat racks, which fold to compact size, make it possible to handle the coats for large crowds. Flexible furniture, which can be used by both adults and children should be provided. This is not as difficult as some might claim since most homes accommodate adults and children in the same facility and do it rather easily. Serious thought should be given to air conditioning for the building. Unfortunately, this is still thought of as a luxury and frequently is omitted from the planning. However, with added usage at night, weekends and particularly summers, such an installation is as feasible as heat in the winter. One might also look at extra facilities such as shops, art rooms, home economics rooms, etc. While these will be found at most secondary schools, they are not always available at elementary schools. It should be kept in mind while planning such facilities that each building does not have to have everything. Duplications in facilities should only be encouraged when there is an absolute need for such duplication.

There are certainly many other things which might be included in planning a building for community specifications. Only some of the most obvious have been mentioned here. Different communities will dictate different things. For example, some communities have taken their pool, cafeteria, gym, and auditoriums, which traditionally are a part of the high school, and have designated them as community facilities. They are on the school site but are viewed as community centers, which the school used at certain hours. Many districts are finding new materials which assist in their planning. New gym materials, for example, make the high school gymnasium a usable place rather than a restrictive shrine. Other communities have discovered that in order to get maximum use of their buildings, they are having to build more traditional types of facilities which will accommodate all ages and then are achieving flexibility through greater use of audio and video technology.

Attention should also be given to existing buildings. While the description to this point has dealt with planning new buildings, the points made and suggestions given apply to existing buildings as well. If present buildings are to serve community needs, then changes will have to be made in these facilities. Generally, this is not as satisfactory as building new facilities, but many communities have made adequate changes in their existing facilities. Usually this means adding to or changing present structures to meet the demands of service to the community. Most of the suggestions can be added to current facilities and the fact that the buildings are already completed should not be an excuse for failing to provide facilities which represent the goals and objectives of the community.

At any rate, the design of facilities with community specifications, while relatively new, is certainly increasing. It has great potential and will certainly mature as it develops. And while there is still much that can happen as communities and architects view this new concept, it is important to keep the basic tenets in mind. Namely, that if schools are to be a moving force in the development of communities and Community Education, they must reflect that concpet in their

School Plant Planning

facilities. Such a reflection will be possible only through design of buildings whose specifications reflect the goals and beliefs of the Community Education philosophy.

CHAPTER XV

Evaluation

The term "evaluation" has certainly moved into the forefront of social concern in the current literature. Not that it has been without significance in the past, but in recent years there seems to be a growing consciousness related to accountability, assessment and other terminology related to evaluating programs and services. And while this phenomenon has been of equal concern to almost all of the segments of our society — business, industry, government, etc. — it has taken on a special significance for education.

In many other areas, i.e., business and industry, evaluation has been a necessary part of the economic cycle. It is mandatory for such enterprises to evaluate their product, their clientele, their management and production techniques in order to operate on a profitable basis. This has been less true, however, for government and education and even though there has often been an awareness of the need for such assessment by these two agencies, little has been done in this direction. In fact, government and education have expended a great deal of energy explaining why evaluation is not possible in their endeavors. Yet, while there certainly is a difference in evaluating products as contrasted with services and while it is easier to assess inanimate objects such as automobiles, can openers, etc., as contrasted with the multi-characteristics and dimensions of people, it is the contention here that evaluation of more subtle and complicated activities, such as education, are possible and desirable and that the problem becomes one of technique rather than one of impossibility.

Definitions

To eliminate the confusion which can develop from semantics, it is probably desirable at this point to define what will be meant by evaluation. There are generally four terms which are used frequently to discuss measurement in education. The first is *assessment.* The term generally refers to the rate or amount of educational components. It might best be identified as an inventory or survey in which data about the education programs is collected without reference to quality or judgment. The second term, *accountability*, is one which is receiving more widespread usage in the recent literature. This term deals with reckoning or answerability. It implies that there is a responsibility for outcomes of education and is primarily used in charging portions of the educational environment (administrators, teachers, boards of education) with the task of delivering demonstrable educational results. The remaining two terms, *appraise* and *evaluation,* are used interchangeably. *Appraise* means to evaluate and *evaluation* implies both examining and judging. Thus, the primary difference between evaluation and assessment is that assessment deals with the more overt task of enumerating and collecting educational information while evaluation not only examines such data but judges it so as to fix a value on such information.

While the field of evaluation is diverse and is applicable to all segments of our social setting, the focus here shall be on evaluation as it pertains to education in general, and to Community Education in particular.

Demand for Educational Evaluation

The educational community is under severe examination and has been for several years. One need only to review current literature to observe the number of critics who have attacked the educational establishment and its methods. In fact, it might be safe to say that no activity has been so severely or continually criticized as education.

There is probably both explanation and justification for these attacks. First of all, the educational institutions of any society play an important part in that society. The literacy, technology, politics, morality, sophistication, artistry and personal attitudes of the society can be influenced and even controlled by the educational system. Subsequently, the educational institutions are the natural object of those who would be desirous of bringing about change or maintaining the status quo within the social setting. Secondly, and closely related to the first, is the "scape-goat" role which education plays in the social setting. Since the school system plays an important part in the education of all members of the community, it becomes the object of criticism for all things that happen within that community and for that matter, all society. It provides a convenient institution on which to focus critical attention in contrast to attempting to place blame on such intangible things as the family or society in general. Unfortunately for education, the school has not only become a preferred target for the social critics, but has become an institution whose public seems over-receptive to negative comments about its operation and function.

A third reason for such criticism comes from the school system itself. Educators for years have made diligent efforts to convince the public of the importance of education. They have attempted to show the importance of literacy, of early childhood education, of the need for continued education and of the relation between education and earning power. And they have been successful. Parents are convinced of the importance of education and have become aggressive in their demands and expectations concerning schools, particularly as they relate to their own children. It is therefore natural to assume that if we constantly stress the importance of education, parents whose children do poorly will develop anxieties and frustrations. Such frustrations often manifest themselves in a dissatisfaction with the school — perhaps even a questioning of the whole educational system.

Another factor in the criticism of education has to do with the financing of education. Financial support of public schools represents the largest expenditure of local and state tax monies and accounts for an increasing expenditure of federal monies. Contrary to other expenditures, such as highway dollars, school monies generally provide facilities for only a portion of the population. Given these conditions, schools become the object of antagonism for those who would like to assault the tax structure of all public expenditures.

Community Education: From Program to Process

Whether these explanations are accurate or not, it still seems evident that schools and educational systems are going to be continually subjected to more demands to prove themselves. For a number of years, the inadequacies of education have been partially overlooked on the basis that the needs of education were being poorly met but there was a kind of tolerance from the public which was in part caused by a public conscience which had been niggardly in its obligations to the schools. This was a period of time when educators had rationalized their shortcomings on the basis of economics. They had pointed to poor salaries, poor facilities and lack of public interest as the reasons why education was not better. In the 1960's, however, compatible state laws regarding negotiations coupled with a more militant profile in the teaching profession resulted in many changes in the economic factors of education. Salaries increased to be commensurate with other professions with equal training. Facilities were greatly improved, and the public conscience for spending at a higher rate for education all tended to ameliorate the public neglect which had existed before.

As things began to change and the overt deficiencies began to be eliminated, or at least improved, a demand rose for the improvements which educators had promised. This demand first showed up in relation to federal funds. Under various legislative actions and titled programs, a large number of dollars was expended in science and math programs, libraries, counseling, poverty and other disadvantaged programs. Federal legislatures now began to request accountability for the funds expended based on not just accounting procedures, but on quantity and quality results. It was not long before state and local governments began to follow suit.

This move by the government has been followed by boards of education, parents, communities and even students. No longer is there a willingness to accept unquestioningly the authority nor the explanations of the professionals within the school setting. Schools have been requested, challenged and now demanded to justify their role and substantiate that which they claim they do. Boards of education are altering their negotiation posture by coming up with demands of their own, and one of the primary demands is for the educators to account for the expenditure of funds which they are receiving. If, for instance, teachers are claiming that higher salaries and tenure result in better teaching and better education, then the public is demanding some evidence of such an outcome. In a like manner, parents are no longer accepting excuses for failure from professionals whose job it is to teach, and community members are expecting justification for the increasing financial support which education is demanding.

As a result, educators suddenly find themselves in need of responding to the demands of accountability. Unfortunately, those who are requesting accountability have discovered that educators do not have accurate means of measuring, assessing, or appraising their product. Because the profession is unable to recommend appropriate measurement procedures, educators have found that their public, particularly the legislators, have proceeded without them. As a result, and much to their consternation, educators find themselves evaluated on the one thing for which they have acknowledged accountability — educational achievement. The result is a strange paradox since achievement is the area on which most educators spend the greatest amount of their time, and yet the one which educators claim should not be the ultimate criteria on which evaluation should be based. The fact is, however, that evaluation, right or wrong, is here to stay, and educators must either take the leadership in identifying what should be evaluated and how the evaluation should proceed, or be willing to accept those instruments and techniques foisted upon them from without.

Educational Evaluation Perspective

The movement toward educational evaluation is not of recent vintage. Evaluation is an outgrowth of the modern testing movement which had its origin in the early 1900's. Between 1900 and 1910 the movement got underway with the work of Joseph Rice in the areas of spelling, intelligence, achievement and basic skills. Between 1910 and 1920 the movement was pushed forward by Thorndike, who introduced such things as objective scoring, scaling of items and established norms. This was also the period when Terman revised the Binet scale. In the 1920's there was additional growth in measurement. Group intelligence scores were developed as well as achievement test batteries. Also, the statistical techniques for analysis became more sophisticated.

The movement to this point has been primarily concerned with the measurement of achievement and intelligence. In the 1930's this direction began to change from one of measurement to one of evaluation. The basis for this movement was that education consists of attempting to meet certain objectives, and achievement was only one of the objectives to be accomplished. In order to look at the total system, it seemed necessary to develop more subtle measures to look at such things as map reading, use of references, and educational indices. There also had to be a concern for attitudes and personality. The idea was to attempt to see the whole individual. New instruments began to appear such as rating scales, questionnaires, judgment scales, interviews, observation techniques, sociometric devices and anecdotal records.

These efforts continued through the 1940's and 1950's. New instrumentation was developed and tests appeared which were designed to measure almost every facet of a person, including aptitudes, educational prediction, and even test awareness. Tests became one of the main criteria for promotion, college admission, scholarships, military placement and employment acceptability.

Unfortunately, these tests still continued to focus primarily on the individual's academic achievement. Tests were and are primarily used to see if the individual is learning what he should. Responsibility for test scores has rarely been placed on the teacher or the school system. Testing is primarily held to be the reflection of either the student's effort, his intelligence, or his heredity and environment.

Some educators, however, have been trying to evaluate more than the individual's outputs. They have insisted that there is a need for accountability by the school system and its staff. They hold that students are the product of that system and that achievement may reflect teaching, expenditures, facilities and many factors other than just the personal characteristics of the student. They claim that school systems and their staffs are responsible for the products which they produce much as any other enterprise is responsible for its products.

Men like Ralph Tyler and Robert Havighurst have been encouraging us for years to do such evaluation. It is their contention that until we look at ourselves and evaluate so that we know our strengths and weaknesses, we shall never be able to make those changes necessary for improving our educational system. They also believe that positive change will not occur until educators accept a major responsible role in the education of the children entrusted to them.

It should be noted here that the evaluation which has come about from federal and state requirements is not motivated by the same reasoning. The thrust from these agencies has been primarily a financial concern. As such, it lacks some of the positive values which evaluation may bring about. Those requesting some evaluation have been primarily concerned with justifying expenditures and consequently seek information which has political significance. Nevertheless, even these requirements have had a positive spin-off since they have tended to create an awareness on the part of the recipients of federal and state dollars that some type of accountability is expected.

The need for evaluation has been concisely expressed by Myron Lieberman when he states that, "The underlying issue is not whether to have accountability, but what kind of accountability will prevail . . . In very broad terms, one approach is through analysis of resources invested related to results achieved . . . . Under this approach, efforts are made to relate input and educational output in some meaningful way . . . . if school systems do not begin to do a better job of relating school costs to educational outcomes, they are likely to be faced with a growing demand for alternatives to public schools . . . . it is difficult to see how public school education could argue this point effectively unless and until they develop more effective ways of being accountable to their patrons." [1]

Let us now try to make these comments about accountability relevant to Community Education. There are probably two comparisons which need to be made. First, in the same way the public schools have not been accountable for their K-12 enterprise, they have not accepted either accountability or responsibility for their other educational responsibilities to the community. Second, the charges being leveled here against the public schools and their failure to assess their traditional programs can also be made against community educators. Community Education programs have made claims for change, but like their counterparts in the K-12 program they have never made the necessary, and in some cases even minimal, effort to demonstrate their effectiveness in terms of whether they have accomplished what they claimed they would accomplish.

---

[1] Myron Liebernam, "An Overview of Accountability," *Phi Delta Kappan,* Vol. LII, No. 4, December, 1970, p. 195.

To be sure, there have been attempts to collect data on Community Education, but in general these efforts have been aimed at the program aspect of Community Education. This information has been collected primarily to satisfy the requirements for annual reports, state reports, and adult and basic education program requirements. The information collected tends to consist of such things as numbers enrolled, number participating, monies collected and spent, teachers employed, rooms used and number of credit and noncredit programs. This kind of data gathering has frequently been called the "numbers game," and while there is value in the collection of such information, it supplies only a limited amount of information on which to make decisions.

In addition to these above-mentioned statistics, there is a need to have information concerning such things as: How is the individual affected personally? What changes in attitude are taking place? What is happening in the area of community problems (crime, delinquency, welfare, etc.)? What are the perceptions of community members about the community? Granted, that while this information will be more difficult to obtain and less objective than statistical data, it is probably much more important to the success of Community Education and is the means by which the very important process aspect of Community Education can be evaluated.

The collection of information of this kind is based on two premises. The first is that perceptions of people are valuable and are a legitimate means of measurement. How a person perceives something is the only true condition to him. No matter what factors are observed by others, you must deal with personal perceptions if you are to evaluate any condition. While this is a very subjective means of gathering information, it is the only evidence which has individual relevance. The second premise is that data other than numbers is available and can be collected, analyzed, and used in evaluation. Data that is not entirely objective is still valid as long as the limitations of the available data are recognized.

If there is other useful data available on Community Education programs and it has not been used, one immediately raises the question, "Why not?" There are several reasons.

Evaluation

The Anti-Ivory Tower Syndrom

Many of the early community educators tended to view their role as one of undoing the evils which the existing educational programs were foisting on the community. They aptly pointed out the failures of schools to meet the need of communities and established their success at the expense of showing the inadequacies of school boards and administrators. This approach gradually resulted in an attitude toward community educators that placed all Community Education on the pragmatic, "gut" level of operation, as opposed to the school-oriented, academic countenance of their adversaries. Traditional educators were classed as being oriented to the training of college-bound students and other scholarly pursuits, of which evaluation and research were important aspects. As a result, there developed within the Community Education movement, a kind of disdain for measurement which made evaluation incompatible with Community Education, at least in the minds of Community Education promoters.

Program vs. Process

As has been pointed out earlier in the test, while Community Education is really comprised of program and process, many Community Education endeavors have stopped far short of total development and consequently are highly program-oriented. With only this much development, a statistical data gathering technique is often sufficient. Where the primary concern is with numbers of people and programs, the data collected generally will be adequate if it accurately determines numbers of people involved.

The Dramatics of Statistics

A part of the success in the expansion of Community Education has been related to this dimension. Numbers are impressive and possess a high degree of influence. People are generally impressed by the number of persons involved and satisfied with outcomes which indicate a high level of participation.

Degree of Difficulty

Collecting evaluative data is an added responsibility. Frequently, the person who accounts for his success by exclaiming that evaluation is useless or that you can feel the results without collecting data is rationalizing his own unwillingness or inability to carry out evaluation responsibilities. If one does decide to gather information, he finds that numbers are easier to collect than more subjective data. He will therefore tend to do that thing which will be most easily accomplished and tabulated. This often results in the establishment of objectives based upon whatever information is easy to collect and whatever programs are easy to evaluate, rather than on what is important to the community.

The Partial Definition

Failure to do a complete job of evaluation sometimes is a reflection of the depth of perception of those who direct the program. A Community Education director who does not thoroughly understand what he is attempting to do will evaluate in terms of his own definition of Community Education. Therefore, if a director perceives Community Education as synonomous with adult education, or recreation, he will tend to collect numbers which support his success in these programs and interpret them as a successful Community Education program. The danger that is evident in evaluation of this type is the problem of ignoring many community needs, while evaluating only what you are doing.

Criteria of Decision-Makers

Much of the evaluation being done is done to answer questions for those who are providing the monies to operate such programs — school boards, state departments of education, universities and foundations. These groups seem to be primarily interested in numbers, and community educators respond accordingly.

Instrumentation

Instruments for measuring Community Education are not abundant. Because of the nature and recency of the concept, test companies and professional evaluators have not developed instruments such as those available to the traditional school programs. The instruments which have been made available have been developed by local districts without much concern or attention to such test characteristics as validity, reliability, scorability, or ease of administration. The reasons why instruments which should measure other aspects of Community Education have not appeared is probably due to difficulty of construction, administration, or lack of motivation to use such devices.

Before looking at evaluation further, it might be wise to differentiate between evaluation and research. The primary difference is the difference between theory and practice. Research deals with the science of education, while evaluation measures the success in practice. Research is concerned with theory, design, and the scientific method as it relates to data collection, methodology and analysis of data. Evaluation, on the other hand, deals with educational problems in a more general way and appraises practical educational activity. The researcher needs a laboratory to exclude all variables other than those being considered. From this he develops basic principles. The evaluator needs to look at these principles in light of the many variables that have an effect in life situations.

How to Evaluate

We have to this point tried to establish a basis for "why evaluate?" In order to carry out a program of evaluation, it is assumed that this rationale has been accepted and that there is support for such action. Unless the top administration and those to be involved support starting such activities, the results may be disappointing. Successful evaluation implies that all involved are desirous of doing a good job and making use of the results. This commitment includes a feeling that by evaluation we will be able to know more about what and how we are doing; where we have been; where we are; and where we are going – a feeling that our programs can never be strong and viable unless we evaluate them accurately and sincerely. We must also acknowledge that the results of our evaluation will establish a base for the kind of direction and change that will take place in our programs of the future.

Once it is evident that there is support for legitimate evaluation, it is then possible to decide how to proceed. It may be at this point, however, that our greatest consternation appears. To say that we have been badly in need of evaluation in the past is an understatement of reality, which more and more is being recognized as an essential part of any productive operation. It has been assumed in the past, however, that the answer lies in more data collection and various types of tests, questionnaires and other collective devices which have been used to assimilate information in what usually ends up to be a disarray of fragmented statistics. Usually, the end result is disagreement among those involved as to the relevancy of the information collected and a great deal of rationalization concerning whether the information does or does not seem to prove some predetermined point which its supporters were hoping it would prove. For example, if measurements showing achievement scores are high then disenchanted portions of the public tend to argue that this shows that schools are only teaching subject matter, have irrelevant curricular and are teaching for the sake of test scores. If such scores are low then the same public points out that this shows the inferior quality of teaching in the schools. In a like fashion, educators tend to claim school responsibility if test scores are high, but if such scores are low, then they point to such factors as heredity, environment, or other nonschool related factors as the cause. As a result, the information collected is generally not used to initiate any change and the whole process of evaluation becomes one of frustration and futility.

The problem illustrated here is often claimed to be one of instrumentation. Basically, the failure is centered within the charge that the wrong things are being measured to judge the quality of the programs and that even those things which are being measured are being measured inaccurately due to the lack of validity and reliability of the instruments being used. Upon these two issues the fate of evaluation has been hanging for a long time and the general assumption has been that if the right instruments could be found which were mutually acceptable to all concerned, then perhaps proper appraisal could be made.

The basic problem is that this conflict over instrumentation is confusing the real issue of the argument. Instrumentation is the outgrowth of a process of evaluation which starts with the selection of goals. As obvious as this might seem, unfortunately, the initial action of goal setting is often overlooked or superficially treated so that evaluators proceed to the measurement aspect of evaluation without first establishing, to the satisfaction of those involved, what things are to be measured. It is true that most school districts do have objectives which have often been established by the board of education. These goals, however, are usually so broad, (i.e., to increase the individual potential of all the students in the school district) and so unpublicized, that there is little relation to what is stated and what is happening in the classrooms.

By the same token, the educational staff must bear its share of guilt in this area. It is amazing to discover how few professional educators are aware of the goals of their school district and how few have ever paused to identify their own personal beliefs about education or what they will try to do in the classroom. And when such efforts have been made, it is alarming to discover how frequently the activities of the class are not related to what the teacher claims are the things that should be happening. In fact, critics place the greatest emphasis in accountability on achievement because, despite claims of interest in citizenship, self-concept, "worthy use of leisure time," health, etc., most classrooms focus all of their attention, including rewards and punishments, on mastery of the academic pursuits.

In transposing what has been said to Community Education, then, the first responsibility in establishing accountability is to decide what the goals of the program should be.

"The underlying concept of the goal-setting approach is simple: the clearer the idea you have of what you want to accomplish, the greater your chance of accomplishing it. Goal-setting, therefore, represents an effort on the part of the management to inhibit the natural tendency of organizational procedures to obscure organizational purposes in the utilization of resources. The central idea is to establish a set of goals for the organization, to integrate individual performance with them, and to relate the rewards system to their accomplishment." [2]

In order to get at goal-setting, it will first be necessary to decide which people should be involved in this part of the process. In general, there are two guidelines to be followed. The first is based upon the

---

[2] Felix M. Lopez, "Accountability in Education," *Phi Delta Kappan*, Vol. LII, No. 4, December, 1970, p. 232.

premise, the greater the input, the more nearly perfect the results. It therefore becomes tantamount that as many people as possible be involved. The second guideline is that there should be input from all segments to be affected by the program. This is to get away from the traditional feeling of being done "to" rather than "with." It is also to bolster a prime axiom of Community Education — involvement. Certainly if a key ingredient within a program is the involvement of people, then there is no better time to accomplish this than at the inception of the program when goals are being established.

In order to best accomplish the involvement, it is suggested that all those who should be involved be identified. This inventory should include such groups as boards of education, administration, teachers, lay citizens, governmental agencies, social agencies, service clubs, churches, and business and industry, with special concern for subgroups within these areas, such as minority groups and special interest areas. Representation from these groups should then be established so that several discussion groups can be identified and activated for the purpose of developing goals and objectives. These groups should be no larger than 20-25 persons each. The goals should be established in terms of priority and should be generally agreed upon by the entire group. The general goals determined at this point are very broad and are designed to provide general direction rather than specific objectives. Once these general goals have been established, it then is necessary to become more specific. These broad, pre-established goals must be analyzed to determine specific concepts within them, to establish more concrete agreement about what the general goal specifically indicates, and to establish basic assumptions inferred in the generalization. This step is an attempt to dissect and analyze the generalized goals that were determined. For example, in Step 1, the group may decide that one of the objectives is to provide formal educational programs for adults. In Step 2, the group will actually itemize what kinds of programs should be included in such a goal, such as high school completion, basic education, avocational classes, recreation programs, etc.

It is important to remember that the establishment of these goals will reflect the group's concept of Community Education. While it is important to share with each group the potential of Community Education, it is also important not to force the establishment of goals which are alien to the group. If the group develops goals which fall short of the anticipated or desired potential of Community Education, it is better to accept this as a need for future education of the community rather than to insist on goals which are neither identified nor comprehended by the group. By accepting group consensus, you are reaching one of the key concepts in Community Education — that of involving and utilizing group process and group decisions.

Before each group disbands, they should select representation to meet with representatives of the other groups. Each of the subsequent groups will be of similar size and will go through the same process as the original groups. The purpose will be to move from a certain number of groups (i.e., 15) to fewer and fewer groups until one final group contains the representation selected by all the previous groups. This group carries with it the input from all of the other groups and will then establish, by consensus, a final set of general goals, arranged in terms of priority with each goal defined in terms of the specific concepts within each. Initially, this part of goal-setting is vital and should be repeated periodically in order to assure that the programs are proceeding as all those affected by the program perceive they should be.

These first two steps provide the basis for overall goals and the specifics expected within the goals by the community to be served. The general question, "What are we trying to accomplish in Community Education?" will have been answered. It now becomes the responsibility of the professionals to implement these goals. In order to do this, a third step is necessary. This step involves the development of performance criteria which are more generally called behavioral objectives. Behavioral objectives have grown out of a concern for accountability. The recent emphasis on Program-Planning Budget Systems (PPBS) is based on the need to relate financial expenditures to the objectives of each program. Under this approach, an organization would break its activities into programs. The objectives for each program would be in terms of things to be accomplished rather than objectives to be purchased. The objectives would be stated behaviorally so that they could be observed and measured. Monies allocated for programs would be based on these objectives and the degree to which the objectives were accomplished would determine future allocations. In order to relate the financing of programs to results, it is necessary to be able to not only develop objectives, but to state them in terms of measurability. Behavioral objectives are those objectives which restate general objectives in terms of actions which can be evaluated.

Community Education: From Program to Process

Behavioral objectives, then, represent an attempt to switch from universal objectives (such as the seven cardinal principles of education) to a more specific, manageable objective. This change is probably an outgrowth of measurement by business, industry and the military. It focuses on both process and product and is precise, observable and measurable.

In establishing traditional objectives, one can only say whether a particular kind of training did or did not occur. It is possible to measure numbers attending, but it is not possible to determine the quality or effectiveness of the program. Changes in individuals will not be measured, and, as a result of improper evaluation, change in the process and output will not take place.

By comparison, behavioral objectives are based on the belief that the product of a program should result in some observable and measurable change in behavior. In preparing behavioral objectives, one should:

1. Decide on who should be affected (entire class, individual, etc.)

2. Decide on what and how much can be accomplished

3. Describe the conditions or means by which success will be measured (personal judgment, test, questionnaire, combination of these)

4. Establish a time limit — when will the things that you want to accomplish be accomplished

This is the goal-setting process which is crucial to proper evaluation, and yet so often is the step which is neglected or treated superficially. Succinctly, it is well-described in the Management by Objectives concept which Lopez describes:

"The program operates within a network of consultative interviews between supervisors and subordinates in which the subordinate receives ample opportunity to participate in the establishment of his own performance objectives. Thus, the whole concept is oriented to a value system based upon the results achieved; and the results must be concrete and measurable . . . .

1. It involves the whole organization in the common purpose.

2. It forces top management to think through its purposes, to review them constantly, to relate the responsibilities of individual units to pre-set goals, and to determine their relative importance.

3. It sets practical work tasks for each individual, holds him accountable for their attainment, and demonstrates clearly how the performance fits into the overall effort.

4. It provides a means of assuring that organization goals are eventually translated into specific tasks for the individual employee.

It is, therefore, virtually impossible to conceive of an effective accountability program that does not operate within the umbrella of the goal-setting process . . . . It insures that subordinate goals and role performances are in support of the goals of the higher levels of the organization and that ultimately the institutional purposes will be achieved . . . . .

This is the essence of results compared to objectives." [3]

Once the behavioral objectives have been established, it is time to decide how best to move the implementation of these objectives. It must be decided what techniques or resources will be used to accomplish the task (lecture, books, movies, group discussions, etc.). This step will provide the input necessary for achieving the tasks described.

Finally, it is time for the evaluation. Since behavioral objectives were decided on in terms of measurability, the techniques for assessment will already have been decided and will be applied at the

---

[3] Ibid. pp. 323-234.

termination of the designated time period. Naturally, it is assumed that the results will be used purposely. The results of any measurement should provide information for determining how well the goals were achieved and what changes should be made in the program for the future.

One question which frequently arises is who should do the measurement. Some prefer to have it done by an outside group. They site advantages such as: Such an arrangement takes away local bias; it is best for sensitive areas, such as racial issues, and has the advantage of bringing in a high level of expertise. On the other hand, there are certain advantages to internal evaluation. For one thing, it is less expensive and frequently it is not so complicated as to require persons with specialized training. One other advantage is that doing your own evaluation brings about an awareness and involvement that is more compatible to change.

Let us summarize the whole area of evaluation by again listing the steps involved and giving examples of each step in the process.

Step I — Establish General Goals

These goals will be established by involving many people in deciding what Community Education should do. Examples of this might be:

A. To provide for the general educational needs of the adult population

B. To make people better members of their community

C. To make the community a better place in which to live.

Step II — Review generalized goals and break them down into smaller parts or basic elements.

Each of the goals listed in the first step would be analyzed to see what specific things might make up such a goal. Using (C) above as an example, some more specific objectives might be:

A. To make community members more conscious of what things are happening in their community

B. To develop a pride in community

C. To improve the appearance of the community.

Step III – Establish behavioral objectives to meet the goals of the specific objectives.

The responsibility for doing this now falls on the professionals responsible for the program. They must analyze how they are doing to carry out their functions in a way which will meet the specific objectives of the program. In the examples cited in Step II, they might include the following behavioral objectives as sub-headings:

1. To make community members more conscious of what things are happening in the community,

    a. Develop a community news organ

    b. Organize the local community for small group discussions

    c. Develop community programs on vital issues

2. To develop a pride in the community,

    a. Offer social activities for the community

    b. Develop some competitive activities with other communities

    c. Provide information about outstanding people, activities, and events within the community.

3. To improve the appearance of the community,

    a. Start fix-up, paint-up projects

    b. Begin community improvement projects, such as landscaping of public buildings and improvement of parks.

    c. Use community influence to get governmental agencies to improve streets, lighting, etc.

In order to complete each of the behavioral objectives listed above, it will be necessary for the professional to include a statement relative to who should be affected, what and how much should be accomplished, the conditions by which success will be measured, and the established time limit for the accomplishment of the objective.

Thus, for the behavioral objective, "Organize the local community for small group discussion," the following information might be included:

1. Will involve at least one discussion group of not less than 20 people from each elementary school community in the school district

2. Will discuss at least four major issues of community interest

3. Success will be determined by reporting on what issues were discussed, the number of participants and the personal observation of each discussion leader.

4. The time period for achieving success shall be one school year, commencing in September and ending in June.

Step IV – Determine Techniques for Achieving Objectives

The professional now must decide how he will implement these established behavioral objectives. He must decide what activities and programs will be used to reach the stated objectives. He will plan these activities and take the responsibility for their development and supervision.

Step V – Evaluation Instrument

Once the behavioral objectives have been established, the means of evaluation can be determined. For example, an item such as the news organ can be evaluated by describing its operation, circulation, composition, and effectiveness in communicating. Formal sessions such as group discussions can be described, documented as to attendance, topic, and number of sessions. Activities in the community also can be described and reported. In order to get a feeling for the quality of a given activity, questionnaires, random opinions of community members and the judgment of professionals can provide information. The form the evaluation will take will depend upon which technique solicits the information relevant to the particular behavioral objective.

The important thing to remember about evaluation related to behavioral objectives is this: general goals have now been reduced to behavioral terms. In other words, goals have been so specifically stated that it is now possible to tell whether such an occurance actually took place. Also, as these objectives have been identified, the form of evaluation has been identified in a similar fashion. Thus, not only is the objective specific, but the evaluation has been described in terms of who is affected, what is to be accomplished, the length of time to be evaluated, and what conditions will determine success. Consequently, by collecting data on these things described, and in the fashion stated, it is possible to decide to what degree the objectives have been accomplished.

In the previous example relating to community discussion groups, it would be possible to enumerate and evaluate those items listed as being necessary for success. It would now be possible to assess whether there had been a discussion group of at least 20 people from each elementary district, to check on the number of topics discussed and to have a report from the discussion leader of each group. Since these things were developed as the behavioral objectives to be achieved, and since the criteria for success was described in definitive terms, the information collected at the end of the time allocated will be both valid and usable for future direction.

The topic of evaluation has been one of much discussion and little activity. It would appear, however, that the day of accountability is upon us and that expectations for more assessment and evaluation will be even greater in the future. The problem which has arisen seems to be one of accepting accountability as a fact-of-life and proceeding to implement the necessary measures. Community Education will be no exception to these expectations — nor should it be. The promoters of Community Education believe in the power of Community Education and have made many claims as to its capabilities. For them to say that it cannot be evaluated is to add confusion to the whole situation. Community Education is a viable concept and can stand the test of evaluation. In fact, good accounting procedures will *prove* the claims which have in the past been supported without evidence. The question then is not *should we evaluate Community Education,* but *how.* The answer seems to lie in developing and following a process for evaluation in terms of goals which are measurable rather than following the haphazard, numerical, techniques of the past.

CHAPTER XVI

The Future of Community Education

Developing predictions about the future is an obviously risky venture. Kenneth Boulding stated the problem well when he said, "One thing we can say about man's future with a great deal of confidence is that it will be more or less surprising." [1]

It is important for educators to attempt to assess the future, however, in an attempt to assure educational relevance; to begin planning for the changes that will be necessitated. In an attempt to do this, this chapter will be divided into three parts:

1. The World of the Future

2. Today's Man in Tomorrow's World

3. Educational Programming of the Future

---

[1] K. Boulding, "Expecting the Unexpected," *Designing Education for the Future,* No. 1, Edited by Edgar Morphet and Charles Ryan; Citation Press, New York, 1967, p. 199.

Community Education: From Program to Process

The World of the Future

"..... two major trends are likely to continue for at least another thirty years: The population will continue to grow, and technology will continue to be a major source of change in the affairs of men."[2] Within these general areas, Robert L. Shinn states that there are five movements presently in operation which will reshape our society.

1. We are presently experiencing a large worldwide population increase. This will present many ethical and social problems to the society. Although technology can expand production to meet the needs of the increased population, there will be a tendency toward increased family planning. This increasing population will create many worldwide ethical and religious conflicts and problems in addition to the technological problem presented by a large population. Many of the beliefs and concepts that we presently hold will have to be rethought.

2. Technology will create broad changes beyond the obvious impact of new inventions and gadgetry. Cybernetics will expand the power of man in ways that we cannot yet perceptualize. Provincialism will become obsolete and problem solving techniques will have to be established to incorporate a much broader perspective. New forms of ethics will have to be considered and developed within an organizational structure, if we are to adequately handle the new technology.

3. The trend toward urbanization will continue, although it will be directed toward suburban living rather than city residence. Large megalopolises will be vested that will change the lifestyle of man to an extent that we cannot yet fathom.

4. The military situation will become increasingly complex. There will be thirty new nuclear powers by 1980. This increases the chances of military disaster but also increases the impulses of man

---

[2] George Miller, "Some Psychological Perspectives in the Year 2000," *Daedalus Journal of the American Academy of Arts and Sciences,* Vol. 96, No. 3, Summer, 1967, p. 884.

for international control. Bertram Russell has written, 'The human race has survived hitherto owing to ignorance and incompetence, but given knowledge and confidence combined with folly, there can be no certainty of survival. Knowledge is power; but, it is powerful for evil as much as for good.'

In any prediction of a future life and a future society, one can only assume that a nuclear holocaust will be avoided and that man can develop the tools necessary to assure this.

5. Human rights will continue to be a major issue. The United States has a tradition of freedom and justice. It now faces the ethical problem of making good that tradition.[3]

Mr. Shinn is obviously pointing to the very serious "human problems" that population growth and technological expansion will bring.

Projections have been made that by the year 2000, seven billion people will share the earth's surface.[4] What will life be like when shared with that many people in a densely populated society that offers little privacy? Man will need greatly increased self-constraint, a new respect for individual differences and customs and an expanded belief in the value of the individual.

Technology will obviously create many problems for human beings along with providing its many services. Shinn mentions the impact of cybernetics briefly. Let us preview this one aspect of technology a little more thoroughly.

---

[3] Robert L. Shinn, "Human Responsibility in the Emerging Society," *Designing Education for the Future,* No. 1, Edited by Edgar Morphet and Charles Ryan; Citation Press, 1967, pp. 243-246.

[4] George Miller, "Some Psychological Perspectives in the Year 2000," *Daedalus Journal of the American Academy of Arts and Sciences,* Vol. 96, No. 3, Summer, 1967, p. 884.

William T. Knox forecasts that the computer will become an extension of the human mind the way the automobile is an extension of the human body. The computer will change life to the same or a greater extent than did the automobile. The automobile left no human institution untouched. The computer will also have this effect. The computer will also be used in revising our present information system. It appears that a reasonable number of direct access computers will store and process all the significant information in the world's libraries. Not only will it be stored; but, computers will be able to talk with the information receiver and organize and manipulate its recorded information to serve the user's needs. Further, it will then store the newly organized data for the other's use.[5]

Many other technological inventions will be developed over the next thirty years. Herman Kahn and Anthony Wiener list one hundred such inventions. Some of these include:

"1   New sources of power for ground transportation (storage-battery, fuel-cell propulsion or support by electromagnetic fields, jet engine, turbine) . . . .

14   Extensive use of cyborg techniques (mechanical aids or substitutes for human organs, sense, limbs) . . . .

16   Relatively effective appetite and weight control . . . .

21   Controlled super-effective relaxation and sleep . . . .

24   Three dimensional photography, illustrations, movies, and televsion . . . .

31   Some control of weather and climate . . . .

33   New and more reliable 'educational' and propaganda techniques for affecting human behavior . . . .

---

[5] William T. Knox, "The New Look for Information Systems," *Designing Education for the Future,* No.1, Edited by Edgar Morphet and Charles Ryan; Citation Press, New York, 1967, p. 223.

35 Human hibernation for relatively extensive periods (months to years) . . . .

40 Capability to choose the sex of an unborn child . . . .

54 Automated grocery and department stores . . . .

55 Extensive use of robots and machines 'slaved' to humans . . . .

58 Chemical methods for improved memory and learning . . . .

69 Individual flying platforms . . . .

84 Home computers to run the household and communicate with outside world . . . .

99 Artificial moons and other methods of lighting large areas at night" [6]

To be able to achieve these technological feats is one thing; to have them foisted upon a society that does not want them, or has not had the chance to decide if they want them is another. Do we really want drugs developed to provide us with the mood appropriate to whatever we are doing? Do we really want an improved capacity to change sex, or the ability to select the sex of an unborn child? What happens to human beings when programmed dreams, mechanical slaves, and chemical methods for improving memory and learning are available?

It seems evident that the world of the future will certainly be different from the one we know today. The forecasting of technological advance is relatively easy. The forecasting of man's capacity to effectively accept and use this technology and control it for his purposes remains open to question. It seems probable that the greatest

---

[6] Herman Kahn and Anthony Wiener, "The Next Thirty-Three Years; A Framework for Speculation," *Daedalus Journal of the American Academy of Arts and Sciences,* Vol. 96, No. 3, Summer, 1967, pp. 711-716.

problem that man will face will not be in creating technological devices but in being able to function as a human being within the technical maze that will be created.

Today's Man in Tomorrow's World

There is little question that the problems that the future will bring are immense. These problems are multiplied by our existing society. At a time when the society needs all of the resources and human potential possible, it is becoming decreasingly capable of handling these problems. Many sociologists fear that America is becoming a mass society — a society which reduces an individual's capacity to truly gain his own identity. The society that this group perceives is one that dehumanizes and depersonalizes individuals; a society which dissolves human difference by attempting to eliminate differences in people. There are several characteristics of the mass society that many sociologists point to as presently existing in America:

1. The loss of a feeling of community and a loss of community conscience

2. The establishment of a mass culture created by the mass media

3. The alienation of individuals from the society, resulting from their individual loss of identity

4. The dissolution of mediating groups and individuals who work between the extremes within the society

5. The growth and development of an institutional bureaucracy that often loses the individual in its immensity and loses its initial purpose for existence to become self-serving and self-perpetuating.

The basic problem within the mass society is the dehumanization that takes place within people. As people become dehumanized, they lose a sense of personal responsibility, a lack of feeling for the larger community, and a lack of acceptance of authority.

At a time when the society most needs uniquely creative and concerned people, it is establishing a system that destroys individuality and diversity. Educators, in preparing for the future, cannot ignore the general direction the society is taking when establishing educational programs that will be relevant to the individual and to the society as a whole.

Educational Programming for the Future

Before we decide where we are going, we should assess where we are and what we are doing. John Goodlad points out that there is little relationship between school success and goals that are claimed as educational aims; that there is an unwillingness on the part of educators to state the purposes to be served by education, schools or specific programs of instruction; that the structure of schools with certain learning coming at specified times is not in concert with our knowledge concerning individual difference and how children learn. Much of our curriculum is justified on no criteria other than habit and tradition. Much of the educational reform being discussed has scarcely touched the teacher in the classroom. Many innovations designed to unshackle the school program are instead tacked on to the school structure. Educators and school systems have a great hesitancy to experiment.

Goodlad feels that by attacking these problems now educational institutions will be able to meet the needs that it will face in the future. To do this, we must develop a sense of purpose within the school; we must bring curriculum change about by careful planning and design.[7] Because we have established no specific goals, generations of students are denied whatever educational program is out of fashion at a particular time. The pendulum swings every 20 years or so in curriculum development and students receive the type of educational program that happens to be in vogue. We must incorporate into the curriculum the problems likely to be facing young adults in the future. Some of these will include population, poverty, polution, technology,

---

[7] John Goodlad, "The Educational Program to 1980 and Beyond," *Designing Education for the Future,* No. 2, Edited by Edgar Morphet and Charles Ryan; Citation Press, New York, 1967, pp. 47-60.

and use of free time. "School guidance people should be taking cognizance of the fact that promising job opportunities for the future appear to be in public health, community service and planning, recreation, conservation, and education."[8] Goodlad also suggests that there will be an increased emphasis on nonremunerative pursuits and that we should attempt to gain a greater balance for cultural and nontotalitarian aspects of the curriculum. Educators must attempt to determine where technology will fit and what can and cannot be automated.

Perhaps the greatest concern of the educator of the future will be in the area of ethics. Ethics are now in an extensive process of change. The major social changes that are coming will provide both an opportunity and a threat. The several major ethical questions that presently face us can result either in an opportunity for or a threat to humanity.

There is at present an undermining of authority. Established authority is losing relevance and there is more demand for experimentation and change. In the future, authority will not be able to exist based only on tradition. The question of affluence and poverty will greatly effect the ethics of the future. Affluence will continue to expand; poverty, if allowed to continue, will create great ethical and political difficulties. We are presently experiencing vast shifts of power. What will happen, both within systems and within world politics as these shifts occur? Major ethical questions will be raised centering on these power shifts. Many questions are being raised concerning individual identity. Will man become a part of a mass culture with a confusion of values and a confusion of identity? Will personal identity and role identity become fused?

We are presently experiencing an increased alienation among people, especially youth. They are moving away from a materialistic society and away from the conformity described by W. H. White and his organization man and David Reeseman's other directed man. We are

---

[8] Ibid, p. 58.

moving apart from the institutions that we have created to assist us. What effects will this have in the future? [9]

There are many specific problems that schools might face and might have to incorporate into the total curriculum. Contraception has reduced fear of pregnancies. This fear often contributed in the past to sexual inhibition, more than did moral beliefs. What should the school's role now become? There are many moral questions raised about drugs that control personality and that cause people to hallucinate. What will the school's role be in this area? We can expect increasingly effective methods of modifying personality and controlling behavior. What will these techniques be? Who will use them? For what purposes? These are questions that should be raised and discussed by the educational institutions.[10]

Developments in molecular biology have raised the possibility that the DNA Code might be radically altered by the substitution of new genetic material. Behavioral modification through genetic control is a distinct possibility. The same questions must be raised — who will control this, who will use it, and for what purposes?

Many observers believe that religion is not as important in our society as it once was. If this is true, and religion is declining as a moral force in our society, what will replace this ethical loss? In a society that will be changing rapidly, perhaps almost daily, the humanities will play an important role and might fill two functions. First, they might provide a tie to the past and encourage a respect for our traditions in past history, which may be extremely important to a highly technological society. Second, they may encourage and promote radical experimentalism in the arts and raise serious pedological questions and encourage creativity. This might be in direct conflict to an increasing trend toward mass culture and mass man.[11]

---

[9] Robert L. Shinn, "Human Responsibility in the Emerging Society," *Designing Education for the Future,* No. 1, Edited by Edgar Morphet and Charles Ryan; Citation Press, 1967, p. 249.

[10] Ibid. pp. 251-252.

[11] Richard Kuhns, Jr., "The Future of the Humanities," *Designing Education for the Future,* No. 1, Edited by Edgar Morphet and Charles Ryan; Citation Press, 1967, pp. 231-242.

It is important that we approach planning for future educational programs cautiously. There is a danger that we can get so wrapped up in our technological advances that we lose sight of the most important things in education. These are things that aren't new or exciting, but things that we have been working toward for a decade in education.

Paul Miller states that five basic goals remain constant:

"1. To learn about self and seek self-realization

2. To learn about others and the art of human relations

3. To learn about economic life, so he may be fed, clothed, sheltered

4. To learn about organized man and his civic responsibility because organized resources — government if you please, make it more certain that self-preservation becomes possible

5. To learn to battle the elements with attendant successes and failures, and thus to become a philosopher to contemplate the purpose of things.[12]

It seems evident that the demands on the educational institution of the future will be extensive. Radical change will be forced upon educators. The vast changes that will occur and be required will require vast expenditures of funds. Unfortunately, it appears that we are approaching, in the immediate future, a period of increasingly inadequate financial assistance for education. This will remain true unless a significant break occurs in attitudes concerning the importance of education. Schools cannot rely on the complex political process required for the passage of millage. This greatly hinders the educational system and its ability to get funds. Present attitudes and funding procedures indicate that our supply of educational services will greatly lag behind the growing demand for them. Modernization of state tax

---

[12] Paul Miller, "Major Implication for Education of Prospective Changes in Society," *Designing Education for the Future,* No. 1, Edited by Edgar Morphet and Charles Ryan; Citation Press, New York, 1967, p. 4

and financial structures need to begin immediately. Local school district financial structures are in need of sharp and prompt revision. Only through initial adequate funding will we be able to begin to plan to meet the needs of the future.

From Program to Process

The educational system and the society as a whole is facing a crisis. Both, it seems, for the same reason. As our educational institutions have grown and developed and as our society has become increasingly organized, structured, and complex, we have left out a very basic element in the structure – the humaneness of man. Man's institutions do not work well for man unless man himself is involved in seeing that they work.

In earlier times, when life was less complicated, people were involved in their government, in their schools, and in their community. They cared about what happened and what did not happen. They were concerned. This is a far cry from the transient, cold, self-seeking society that we presently have.

Recognizing this, the schools must initiate a transition back to some very basic elements within a democratic society. Democracy requires involvement – it cannot survive without it. We must turn our attention back to local human involvement in very basic issues and problems if we are to survive. Leadership for this move, should logically come from the schools. Educators must begin now to involve community members in planning their own destiny.

Community Education in the future must be established on the premise that people must be involved in community decisions that affect them; on process rather than program. For if Community Education remains committed only to providing program opportunities and not providing problem-solving and involvement opportunites, it will fail. Education must become what former President Lyndon Johnson foresaw when he stated:

> "Tomorrow's school will be a school without walls – a school built of doors which open to the entire community. Tomorrow's school will reach out to places that enrich the human spirit; to the

Community Education: From Program to Process

museums, to the theaters, to the art galleries, to the parks and rivers, and mountains.... Tomorrow's school will be the center of community life for grownups as well as children, as shopping centers for human services. It might have a community health clinic or public library, a theater and recreation facilities for all citizens — and it will not close its doors anymore at 3 o'clock. It will employ its buildings around the clock, its teachers around the year. We just cannot afford to have an $85 billion plant in this country open less than 30 percent of the time."[13],

Compare this to the description of public education presented by the Education Policy Commission:

"Place: An American High School
Setting: A democracy struggling against strangulation in an era marked by confused loyalties in the political realm, by unrest and deprivation, by much unnecessary ill health, by high pressure propaganda, by war and the threats of war, by many broken or ill-adjusted homes, by foolish spending, by high crime rates, by bad housing, and by a myriad of other urgent, real human problems. And what are the children in this school, in this age, in this culture, learning? They are learning that the square of the sum of two numbers equals the sum of their squares plus twice their product; that Millard Fillmore was the thirteenth President of the U.S. and held office from January 10, 1850 to March 4, 1853; that the capital of Honduras is Tegucigalpa; that there were two Peloponnesian Wars and three Punic Wars; that Latin verbs meaning command, obey, please, displease, serve, resist, and the like take the dative; and that a gerund is a neuter verbal noun used in the oblique cases of the singular and governing the same case as the verb."[14]

The decision as to which direction education takes — which road we follow — will be made by that small group of dedicated people who believe in Community Education. They will make the decision to work

---

[13] President Lyndon Johnson at A.A.S.A., Convention, Atlantic City, New Jersey, 1966.

[14] Education Policies Commission, *The Purposes of Education in American Democracy*, National Education Association, Washington D. C., 1938, pp. 146-47.

like they have never worked before and they will accomplish the lofty goals Community Education can reach. Or, they will let the opportunity slide past because of inaction, timidity, or lack of human compassion, and our very democracy will be treatened as a result. The decision must be made — it must be made now.